The Anatomy of Evil

Charles W. Conn

Fleming H. Revell Company
Old Tappan, New Jersey

Library of Congress Cataloging in Publication Data

Conn, Charles W
   The anatomy of evil.

   Bibliography: p.
   1. Devil   2. Devil—History of doctrines.
I. Title.
BT981.C64   235′.47   80–21103
ISBN 0–8007–1177–7

FOR Dorcas Watson

my friend . . .
a woman of good works

Contents

Foreword

Charles W. Conn has ministered to me most effectively through his previous books. I find that he writes clearly and with deep consideration and love. He writes about the things that matter in a way that I can understand and be inspired by them.

I am especially happy to have read *The Anatomy of Evil.* This is a book that we have needed very much. I hear and read various discussions by ministers and others on the general theme of evil in the world. Unless one is careful, one may become confused.

There is much evil in this world. It seems that in many instances, the evil is increasing. Who causes evil? What are the reasons for evil? How can we live with the thought that evil is all around us? What can we do about it? These are some of the questions that we all face and in this book we get some very substantial answers.

I have great admiration and appreciation for the insights of Charles W. Conn. Often, some indignant reader will write me, saying that he or she read a sentence in one of my books with which they disagreed. I always write back, "Thank God I was able to write a sentence that caused you to think enough that you were willing to write me a letter." *The Anatomy of Evil* will cause a lot of thinking, and maybe even some letters to the author, and that would be beneficial.

I feel this book makes a substantial contribution and I am grateful for it.

CHARLES L. ALLEN

Preface

We live in a time that is both troubled and troubling—when even the mundane occupation of reading the daily news can be a bewildering experience. Modern man has somehow managed to live with the ordinary and familiar evils, such as widespread crime, natural disaster, and human tragedy; he has learned to cope with the ills of modernity, such as runaway inflation, material shortages, sexual confusion, and family fragmentation. But now some new and disturbing elements have been added to the contemporary scene with the resurgence of the occult, sorcery, demonism, satanism, and numerous other twisted cults. Man is ill-equipped to handle these dark shadows in his world, much less their terrible offshoots: religious terrorism, murderous messiahs, and national diabolism.

It is easy, therefore, for modern man to feel that his world is on the verge of chaos—out of control, ungoverned and ungovernable—but such an impression is inaccurate, born of fear and encouraged by ignorance of God's Word. In Scripture, we can discover the causes of the present bewildering evil and discern the pattern of diabolical influence in the world. Unfortunately, however, even Christian men are frequently afraid of the subject of Satan and avoid it as something negative and unhappy. In so doing, they perpetuate both man's historical fear of Satan and certain misconceptions about his works.

In truth, a satanic conspiracy is afoot today, with fear and confusion among its prime objectives. Furthermore, we should know that Satan's earliest scheme of evil will be asserted in full strength just before the end of this age. Such modern problems as social injustice, the drug culture, the hippie wave, the Moonies, and the Children of God, and such men as Adolf Hitler, Idi Amin, Charles Manson, Father Divine, and Jim Jones—some vile, some merely deluded—are all alike in one important aspect: They are pawns of Satan in his master plan for the world.

The same is true of the more recent epidemic of terrorism in the name of socio-religious causes, and the holding of hostages with the sanction of—or even at the behest of!—religious leaders. None of these events should be viewed in isolation, for all are somber pieces in the puzzle of the last days.

This is a book of instruction and consolation for our troubled times. Although it concerns the scheme of Satan that has existed since the dawn of time, it is not a book about him. Although it deals sometimes with sensational subjects, it is not intended to titillate sensation seekers. Instead, it proposes to provide enlightenment about certain confusing events of our time, and introduce a measure of reassurance into that confusion.

Its technique is to explore the tangled scene in the light of holy Scripture. When we do this, we find the consolation we need, as well as the reassurance that God is still in control of His universe, and that His will shall prevail in the end. That, of course, is the confidence of all Christian believers.

Several persons have assisted me in the preparation of the manuscript. Principal among them are Mrs. Evaline Echols, my administrative assistant and secretary for the past decade; Mrs. Camilla Warren, my daughter and secretarial assistant; and Mrs. Lucille Walker, who graciously read the completed manuscript and offered valuable suggestions. Most of all, I appreciate my lovely wife, Edna, whose genius for managing me a home and ingenuity in shielding her husband from its distractions make it possible for me to write at all.

CHARLES W. CONN
Cleveland, Tennessee

PART I
The Intention of Satan

1

Is There a Devil?

On a mountaintop high above an ancient European city, a massive medieval castle looms stark and brooding against the sky. Built centuries ago as a religious fortress, a center of the Counter-Reformation, the castle's cold, dark interior is filled with religious emblems and artifacts. Except for the instruments of torture once used to extract confessions and gain "conversions," the most prominent symbols in the fortress relate in one way or another to the devil. With dungeons and darkened corridors a world apart from the warm Austrian sun outside, deaf to euphonies of Mozart or the happy music festivals of today, the fortress is a gloomy monument to man's benighted past.

In that far-off time when the castle was alive and active, the devil was seen as a real and present force of evil, with powers almost equal to God's. That is what medieval man believed . . . and he was filled with fear.

Satan was depicted in symbol and effigy as lord of the underworld, sovereign of hell. He was portrayed as a horned, goat-headed fiend, scowling among a frightening assortment of demons, witches, and evil spirits. Superstitious men trembled at the very thought of such a terrifying assemblage of evil powers, and the worst possible fate that could befall a man was to be possessed: taken over, body and soul, by an evil spirit. Demons were believed capable of rending or tormenting their human victims—or, worse still, of transforming them into violent, sinister creatures of bestial nature. The mood of the times was a nightmarish amalgam of truth and superstition, with demons, witches, vampires, were-

wolves, and other frightful monsters accepted as equally real
and ready at any moment to snatch away the unwary, un-
guarded soul.

To ward off malevolent spirits, men wore on their persons
or displayed on their premises a mysterious collection of fe-
tishes, amulets, and charms. The more superstitious used po-
tions, brews, and concoctions to protect themselves from the
omnipresent demonic horde.

In spite of all that men tried to do to prevent it, however,
evidence of the feared demon possession was everywhere. To
the medieval mind, demons were behind such sicknesses as
asthma, epilepsy, and dropsy. Demons were behind most er-
ratic behavior, too; aberrant dreams; and—especially—the
"evil eye." Almost everything that could not be understood
or explained in the simplest way was reckoned to be the work
of the devil, or of one of his vile agents.

Disbelief in Satan

Gradually, men became more analytical and critical of
their beliefs—more scientific in their knowledge, and less
frightened by the unseen. In revulsion against the former ex-
travagant superstition and terror, enlightened men re-
jected the idea of a devil altogether. Satan became only a
word, a superstition—the figment of a bygone fear: There
was no place for him in "modern" thinking. An actual devil
had no part in a world of psychology, test tubes, and modern
technology. Too much was known about psychoanalysis and
the sicknesses of body and mind now for anyone to take the
devil seriously, and belief in him was swept away—as so
much litter from one of the new antiseptic hospital wards—
by scientific knowledge and modern theology.

The devil was now depicted in cynical caricature, with
stubby horns, a spearlike tail, a mischievous goatee, and a
pitchfork in hand. No one could really believe in or fear such

a devil. The agents of the devil—demons, witches, and the like—were discarded along with him, or, better yet, transformed into childish pranksters at Halloween (or more recently into lovable subjects of playful television comedies). Yes, for the most part, the idea of a devil became great fun.

Persistent Evil

But now, even modern man knows that his world is actually filled with evil—undeniable evil—inexplicable, irreconcilable evil that is not fazed by social improvement, educational advancement, or medical marvels. On the contrary, instead of being made better by his advantages, man has generally become worse. Rampant violence makes mockery of his noblest intentions. Spiritual confusion and ignorance ignore his vaunted knowledge and understanding. Evil grows like weeds in the finest gardens of the twentieth century. Faced by forces beyond his comprehension, man has slowly returned to the realization that there must be a devil, after all.

In our day, there has been an awakened awareness of Satan. Generally, this renewed emphasis has come from Christian pulpits and the pages of Christian literature. But the concern extends far beyond that: There has come the terrible realization that, behind the evil conditions in the world, there must be a power not *of* this world.

This consciousness has been dramatically emphasized in a plethora of popular books about the devil and demon possession, such as *The Exorcist,* and in the motion pictures made from those books. Fascination with devil-related themes is big business for Hollywood and the paperback trade. And scenes like this happen every day:

Under the glaring white lights of a movie marquee, a rush of youngsters leaves the theater where they have just seen a Hollywood depiction of demonic possession. In a ripple of excitement, there are expressions of fear and fantasy (but hardly a word of comprehension). There is the thrill of fear and incomprehension—as if they had seen a dreadful fairy tale, or some strange fable from the pages of science fiction, or even the inside of a drug-induced trip.

For, to be sure, an accurate awareness of the devil and demonic presence is still beyond the understanding of modern man. Worse yet, he has little assurance regarding the limitations of Satan's power. The idea that a devil exists, with the power to control or influence human beings, is offensive to the modern mind. Yet thinking men of this generation are forced to correlate the unmistakable evil around them with traditional notions about the devil and his work.

Some who see and believe are Christians who have grown lax in their dedication, but who yet retain a vague understanding of Satan's power. They know the frightful possibilities—and they are filled with fear. Once again, their fear becomes an unreasoning dread, based upon inaccurate beliefs. The shock of hearing that a devil can possess a human being is too much for most modern men. So some hold to callous disbelief, while others are stricken with fear.

Both reactions are wrong.

Terror of Our Times

Is there a devil? That question needs an honest answer.

Consider for a moment what great evil can and does happen in our time. What besides the existence of a devil can explain how seemingly civilized, educated men, such as the Nazis in World War II, could systematically slaughter and destroy their fellowmen in an effort to exterminate a race? What besides demonic inspiration can create a Dachau, a Belsen, a Buchenwald, an Auschwitz? How, without a devil, can we explain the methodical combination of science and savagery, gas ovens and "final solution," that effected the remorseless destruction of six million human beings?

What besides a devil can cause the horrors of godless political massacres that have become commonplace in our time? How, but by demonic motivation, can a perverted, brutal Ugandan, Idi Amin, amuse himself with the sanguinary murder of 300,000 of his countrymen? What sense or reason can inspire a man to such debauched entertainments and brutality, such lust for blood, such contempt for human life and dignity?

How else can we fathom the atrocities of Pol Pot, turning his country into a morass of blood with the slaughter of an estimated 1 million Cambodians? What can account for such dimensions of evil, except the inspiration of Satan?

What but Satan's influence, shocking and sorrowful as it is, can lead 913 hungry, misplaced souls into an orgy of death in a squalid Guyanese "utopia"? Who else would inspire men and women to pour deadly poison down the throats of defenseless infants and wrinkled elders, beguiled into believing that there was a glory in the dying?

Unfortunately, these manifestations of evil are of such a grand scale that individual man is inclined to disassociate himself from them. So let us look at what simple and insignificant man is capable of doing.

One highly publicized outrage concerns a "family" of youths, their minds twisted by drugs, venereal disease, and sexual profligacy. Driven by the messianic madness of their leader, Charles Manson, hell-bent on destruction and murder, the youths raged from their desert den to kill, wantonly and without pity. They killed an unborn child in its mother's womb, even as they killed the pleading mother. Equally mercilessly, they killed others on their rampage of violence. In a two-night ritual of butchery, they murdered seven persons, inflicting 169 separate stab wounds; stuck a knife in one victim's throat, a fork in his stomach—then carved the word *war* in the still-warm flesh of his body. They scrawled cryptic messages on the walls with the blood of the dead.

All of this was done at the behest of a man maddened to

the point of pretended deity—and without an expression of regret, without a pang of conscience, without the slightest comprehension of what they had done. It was as if the murderers had no mind or thought of their own—or as if what thought they did have was unspeakably cruel and savage.

Every day of our lives, there are less-celebrated incidents that show the modern influence of Satan. Recently, for example, a band of wasted young men, loitering like animals in a city park, seized upon a young cripple walking home from selling papers, and, mindlessly, without reason, stabbed him until his life was gone. One of the assailants muttered to the dying youth, "Thanks," as he drew his bloody knife from the victim's breast. The young murderer, with his twisted sense of gratitude to the victim, seemed to have satisfied an irresistible urge to kill.

Two young women, pretty enough in appearance, went on a killing spree. When one victim lay dead at their feet, one of the girls senselessly dug her spiked heel into the dead man's face, twisted her heel until the dead flesh was torn from the cheekbones, and chortled with glee, "I love this. This is really living."

A young couple and their two children went on a quiet, peaceful family picnic. After the husband spread the food on the ground, his toddling son stumbled into it. The father became enraged, and knocked the baby to the ground. Then, as if possessed, he dashed the broken body of his infant son against trees, stumps, stones. His fury spent, the father wept, cuddled the lifeless body to his breast, and said, "I wanted you to enjoy the picnic."

A father became so angry when his little stepdaughter wet her bed that he punished her in strange, inhuman ways. He made the child walk hour after hour, day and night; beat her with a club; and taunted her thirst by giving her a vile, hot sauce to drink. He heaped unfeeling abuse upon the child until she finally fell exhausted upon her pad on the floor and died.

An unkempt and disheveled young man stormed and raged at his grieving parents, accusing and abusing them with an outburst of venom. He denounced them, and wished them dead. The rebel son repaid their love with spite, as he stormed from the comforts of home to the miseries of alcoholism and drug addiction. (How often this happens in our time!)

Vandals set upon the sacred precincts of a church, stole everything of value that could be moved—then desecrated the sanctuary with offal. Leaving conspicuous evidences of a sexual orgy on the altar, they scrawled obscenities along the walls and even across the pages of the Bible.

Not a day of our time passes but such inexplicable incidents happen, somewhere, in some part of the world. The news of each day has become a sickening record of the depths to which man has sunk.

Is there a devil?

The answer is clearly, Yes, there *must* be a devil. Behind the terror of our times there has to be a demonic power. We cannot discover or understand this fact through human reasoning or scientific investigation. We must, therefore, brush aside mistaken concepts of Satan and look forthrightly at what God tells us about him in His Word.

Satan is a deceiver, whose scheme is to confuse and distort the truth, even about himself. He would have us believe that he is no more than a good-natured spirit who enjoys pulling pranks on human beings. Or, contrariwise, he would have us believe he has more power than he actually has. It pleases him when he can strike such terror to the human heart that men cower in fear before, and strive to pacify him. Misunderstanding, confusion, and disorder are the handiwork of the devil; they create the atmosphere in which he does his serious work.

Because the Word of God clearly identifies the devil and exposes his mad intention, we must look to the Scriptures for our enlightenment and assurance. In the course of these pages, we will see what God says about the devil. What does Satan really want, and how is he going after it? And what about us Christians? What should our position be in the midst of the satanic plot?

We need to know.

2

Nature of the Mystery

The Apostle Paul warned the Thessalonian Christians about the troubled circumstances that will prevail at the end of this age. Since the purpose of his writing was to reassure the believers, though, Paul encouraged them to "be not soon shaken in mind, or be troubled," but to be established "in every good word and work."

What Paul revealed to the Thessalonians is disturbing news about the scheme of Satan; and yet it was necessary that the revelation be made. He called the scheme a *mystery*—"the mystery of iniquity."

The Mystery Revealed

The entire second chapter of 2 Thessalonians should be read thoughtfully. It is both a revelation of the operation of Satan, and a source of spiritual encouragement to those who are in Christ Jesus. For the purposes of our study, we shall look at only the first seven verses:

Now we beseech you, brethren, by the coming of our Lord Jesus Christ, and by our gathering together unto him, That ye be not soon shaken in mind, or be troubled, neither by spirit, nor by word, nor by letter as from us, as that the day of Christ is at hand. Let no man deceive you by any means: for that day shall not come, except there come a falling away first, and that man of sin be revealed, the son of perdition; Who opposeth and exalteth himself above all that is called God, or that is worshipped; so that he as God sitteth in the temple of God, shewing himself that he is God. Remember ye not, that, when I was yet with you, I told you these things? And now ye know what withholdeth that he might be revealed in his time. For the *mystery of iniquity* doth already work: only he who now letteth will let, until he be taken out of the way.

2 Thessalonians 2:1–7, emphasis added

Paul's use of the word *mystery* is significant. In its common sense, it suggests something obscure, hidden, and incomprehensible—something strange and unknown, with a tantalizing quality in its very unknowability. Scriptural usage of the word *mystery,* however, is somewhat different. It is not found in the Old Testament at all, yet we find it used twenty-seven times in the New, where it refers to some fact or knowledge that God shares with His people. A mystery, in this sense, is that which is not intellectually known or generally understood, but is revealed by Christ to those who serve Him.

This is one of the many benefits of the Christian life. God does not leave us in the dark regarding His works or His plans; He freely shares with us His knowledge and the details of His operation on earth. A mystery, then, is *a previously hidden truth now revealed by the Spirit of God.* Obviously, then, the mystery is revealed only to those who accept and believe the Word of God. Consequently, while ungodly men remain ignorant of revealed truth, those who believe the Word of God can be knowledgeable regarding it.

This supernatural revelation comes by spiritual acceptance as well as intellectual comprehension. We must believe and accept the holy Scriptures as the Word of God. By doing this, Christians are able to understand great truths that the rest of the world is unable to grasp. It is in this connection that Paul said:

Now to him that is of power to stablish you according to my gospel, and the preaching of Jesus Christ, according to the *revelation of the mystery,* which was *kept secret* since the world began, But now is *made manifest,* and by the scriptures of the prophets, according to the commandment of the everlasting God, made known to all nations for the obedience of faith.

Romans 16:25, 26, emphasis added

Howbeit we speak wisdom among them that are perfect: yet not the wisdom of this world, nor of the princes of this world, that come to nought: But we speak the *wisdom of God* in a *mystery*, even the *hidden wisdom*, which God ordained before the world unto our glory: Which none of the princes of this world knew: for had they known it, they would not have crucified the Lord of glory.

1 Corinthians 2:6–8, emphasis added

God's Great Mysteries

There are eleven great mysteries, or revealed truths, developed in the Scriptures for our understanding. They are as follows:

The mysteries of the kingdom of heaven. In a series of seven parables (Matthew 13:3–48), Jesus gave what are called mysteries of the kingdom of heaven: the sower and his seed; the tares among wheat; the grain of mustard seed; the leaven of the bread; the hidden treasure; the pearl of great price; and the fisherman's net.

When Jesus' disciples asked why He spoke to them in parables, He answered, "Because it is given unto you to know the *mysteries* of the kingdom of heaven, but to them it is not given. . . . Therefore speak I to them in parables: because they seeing see not; and hearing they hear not, neither do they understand" (Matthew 13:11, 13, emphasis added). He went on to say that even the prophets were not privy to all the things made known to Christians.

The mystery of the translation of the living saints at the end of the church age. We refer to this event as The Rapture—the time when Jesus shall catch His people away from the earth to be with Him in the heavens. The secular world has no comprehension of this fact, yet it is one of the most comforting and reassuring expectations of Christians. "Behold, I shew you a *mystery;* We shall not all sleep, but we shall all be changed, In a moment, in the twinkling of an eye, at the last trump: for the trumpet shall sound, and the dead shall be raised incorruptible, and we shall be changed" (1 Corinthians 15:51, 52, emphasis added).

The mystery of the Church as the body of Christ, composed of Christian Jews and Gentiles of this age. "By *revelation* he made known unto me the *mystery.* . . . Unto me, who am less than the least of all saints, is this grace given, that I should preach among the Gentiles the unsearchable riches of Christ; And to make all men see what is the fellowship of the *mystery,* which from the beginning of the world hath been hid in God, who created all things by Jesus Christ" (Ephesians 3:3, 8, 9, emphasis added).

The mystery of the Church as the bride of Christ. After Paul speaks of how husbands should love their wives—even as they love themselves, forsaking all others for their wives' sake, so that two become one—the apostle adds, "This is a great *mystery:* but I speak concerning Christ and the church" (Ephesians 5:32, emphasis added).

The mystery of the in-living Christ. "Even the mystery which hath been hid from ages and from generations, but now is made manifest to his saints: To whom God would make known what is the riches of the glory of this *mystery* among the Gentiles; which is Christ in you, the hope of glory" (Colossians 1:26, 27, emphasis added).

The mystery of the Godhead. This, perhaps the greatest of all mysteries, reveals that the fullness of the Godhead dwelt bodily in the Lord Jesus Christ. "That their hearts might be comforted, being knit together in love, and unto all riches of the full assurance of understanding, to the acknowledgement of the *mystery of God,* and of the Father, and of Christ; In whom are hid all the treasures of wisdom and knowledge. . . . For in him dwelleth all the fulness of the Godhead bodily" (Colossians 2:2, 3, 9, emphasis added).

The mystery of godliness. This is that truth by means of which man is restored to godliness through the sacrifice of the Lord Jesus Christ. "And without controversy great is the *mystery of godliness:* God was manifest in the flesh, justified in the Spirit, seen of angels, preached unto the Gentiles, believed on in the world, received up into glory" (1 Timothy 3:16, emphasis added).

The mystery of Israel's blindness to the Gospel of Jesus Christ. "For if thou wert cut out of the olive tree which is wild by nature, and wert graffed contrary to nature into a good olive tree: how much more shall these, which be the natural branches, be graffed into their own olive tree? For I would not, brethren, that ye should be ignorant of this *mystery,* lest ye should be wise in your own conceits; that blindness in part is happened to Israel, until the fulness of the Gentiles be come in" (Romans 11:24, 25, emphasis added).

The mystery of the seven stars. "The *mystery* of the seven stars which thou sawest in my right hand, and the seven golden candlesticks. The seven stars are the angels of the seven churches: and the seven candlesticks which thou sawest are the seven churches" (Revelation 1:20, emphasis added). In this mystery, we see how an element of the supernatural remains even after something formerly hidden is made known. It is necessary to understand John's imagery of stars, angels, and candlesticks. The stars represent angels—not celestial angels, but *messengers* (very possibly the preachers of the seven churches).

The mystery of Babylon. The name Babylon is given to a system of apostate religion that will flourish in the last days. It is characterized as a harlot. This mystery will be important to us as we continue our study of apostasy and iniquity. "And upon her forehead was a name written, MYSTERY, BABYLON THE GREAT, THE MOTHER OF HARLOTS AND ABOMINATIONS OF THE EARTH. And I saw the woman drunken with the blood of the saints, and with the blood of the martyrs of Jesus: and when I saw her, I wondered with great admiration. And the angel said unto me, Wherefore didst thou marvel? I will tell thee the *mystery*

of the woman, and of the beast that carrieth her, which hath
the seven heads and ten horns" (Revelation 17:5–7, emphasis
added).

The mystery of iniquity. Development of this important revelation runs through much of the New Testament. Paul emphasized that the mystery was already at work in his day (2
Thessalonians 2:7), but that it will increase and intensify
until its culmination in the last days. This is the revelation of
truth that, depressing though it is at times, we now propose
to trace from its beginning to the present time.

Kinds of Sin

Anyone who reads the Scriptures—either the Old Testament or the New—becomes aware of the word *iniquity.* In a
cursory reading, one gets the impression that iniquity is
wrong—a grievous sin of some kind. The tendency, as understandable as it is erroneous, is to interpret all degrees and
types of sin as the same thing. They are not. Nor are the
terms for sin strictly synonymous. It is important in this
study that we recognize iniquity as a specific, particular type
of sin—more serious than mere transgression or disobedience. To that end, let us note the subtle differences of the
terms:

Sin. The word *sin,* which is generic and all-encompassing,
is by far the most comprehensive term for matters of unrigh-
teousness; it refers to all forms of spiritual guilt and error. Sin
is a lack of conformity to, or transgression of, the law of God.
"Sin is the transgression of the law" (1 John 3:4); "All un-
righteousness is sin . . ." (1 John 5:17); "Whatsoever is not of
faith is sin" (Romans 14:23).

Within the broad meaning of the word *sin,* it is added that
"All have sinned, and come short of the glory of God"
(Romans 3:23); and "If we say that we have no sin, we deceive ourselves, and the truth is not in us" (1 John 1:8). It
should also be understood that there are degrees of sin.

"There is a sin unto death. . . . there is a sin not unto death" (1 John 5:16, 17). It is easy to see, then, that sin is any act or circumstance that is contrary to the will of God for man.

Transgression. Of the several scriptural terms that refer to violations of God's law, the most precise is *transgression,* which is simple disobedience of the law—the active violation of a standard set by God. "Where no law is, there is no transgression" (Romans 4:15). We therefore read about Adam's transgression, for example, which introduced sin into the world (Romans 5:14); and that Jesus was crucified between men who had transgressed the law (Mark 15:27, 28).

Neglect. Not only is active transgression of the law a sin, but so is the willful neglect of that which is good. Referred to as sins of omission, such failures to do good are lapses of character or failures to seize opportunity that must be classified as sin. "Therefore to him that knoweth to do good, and doeth it not, to him it is sin" (James 4:17). Although James states it most succinctly, the sin of neglect is also seen in the absence of love (1 John 3:10) and in the absence of faith (Romans 14:23). The principle of sin by neglect is found everywhere in Scripture—for example, the loss of light by insufficient preparation (Matthew 25:1–12); the burying of the talent (Matthew 25:24–26); and the neglect of God-given ability (1 Timothy 4:14).

Iniquity. If the word *sin* is general, as the word *tree* is general, then, the word *iniquity* is specific, as *elm* or *oak, pine* or *cedar.* More devilish than mere transgression, iniquity is both the center and extreme of sin. Its distinction is first suggested when it is mentioned along with—and in addition to—transgression: "But he was wounded for our transgressions, he was bruised for our iniquities . . ." (Isaiah 53:5).

Fifteen root words are translated *iniquity* in the English-language Bible, which tells us something about the subtle aspects of this sin. It is of great significance that *all appearances of iniquity have to do with religion*—perversion of the truth, overt rebellion against God, rejection of divine law, or the substitution of a counterfeit law. Iniquity embodies deceit—evil in the cloak of righteousness; crookedness and pretense in one's religious life.

To be more explicit, iniquity is perverse, harmful disobedience in religious people. Those accused of iniquity are invariably persons with claims of supposed righteousness that do not square with their lives of sin. Sinners usually commit sin without pretense of religion; transgressors violate God's law without masks of piety; but iniquitous men are evil men who make the claim or have the name of being good. "And because inquity shall abound, the love of many shall wax cold" (Matthew 24:12). This is why Jesus showed compassion toward transgressors and sinners, but was angry with and severe toward workers of iniquity.

Workers of Iniquity

The people of Israel, because of a special relationship with God, had a godly heritage and claim that made them a select nation. Sins in Israel were, therefore, frequently designated iniquity. "But when the righteous turneth away from his righteousness, and committeth iniquity, and doeth according to all the abominations that the wicked man doeth, shall he live? All his righteousness that he hath done shall not be mentioned: in his trespass that he hath trespassed, and in his sin that he hath sinned, in them shall he die" (Ezekiel 18:24).

Judas Iscariot, one of the Twelve, partaker of the holy Gospel, commissioned by Christ, was the most infamous worker of iniquity in the New Testament—or, for that matter, of all time (Acts 1:18). He who should have been better than the other men of his time was worse. Much worse.

Simon Magus, a Jewish sorcerer with wide claims of being a man of God—and, finally a pretended convert to Christianity—was bound by iniquity (Acts 8:23). He so mixed the bad and the good that, eventually, he became confused himself.

The Pharisees, once a noble and worthy company who

maintained the faith of Israel in the dark days before the Lord came, were gradually filled with oppressive self-righteousness. By the time Jesus encountered them, they were His worst enemies—dedicated obstructionists of the kingdom of God. He said of them, "Even so ye also outwardly appear righteous unto men, but within ye are full of hypocrisy and iniquity" (Matthew 23:28).

The Scarlet Woman, an apostate religious system in the last days, will be filled with such sin and iniquity that God will bring judgment upon her. "For her sins have reached unto heaven, and God hath remembered her iniquities" (Revelation 18:5). The Scarlet Woman, by whose sorceries all nations will be deceived, will embody Satan's final pose of righteousness before the end of the age.

Collectively, the work of iniquity forms a dark weave of religion without God, without Christ, without righteousness. It would remove the worship of God, by subtlety or force— by whatever effective means it can—and replace it with the worship of another. The whole mad scheme of iniquity, in the present as in the past, with its intricate use of deceit and violence, stems from the earliest enterprise of Satan—that enterprise, in fact, that made him the devil.

3

The Platform of Lucifer

The devil was not always a devil. On the contrary, there was a time when he was a bright part of the heavenly host, known as "Son of the morning" and noted for his wisdom and beauty. It is indicated in Scripture that his name, Lucifer, was once as honorable as those two other familiar angelic names, Michael and Gabriel. Other names occur in the Jewish compilation of archangels—Raphael, Uriel, Chamuel, Jophiel, and Zadkiel—but these are apocryphal, not found in Scripture. We know almost nothing about the angelic orgnization of heaven, particularly before the rebellion of Lucifer, but we do have an adequate record of what happened to change a lofty angel into the devil.

His Origins

Ezekiel 28:2–19 and Isaiah 14:12–17 give us significant views of Lucifer in that far-off time before sin entered his heart and he became Satan. In Ezekiel's account he is said to have been: full of wisdom; perfect in beauty; perfect in his ways; an anointed and covering cherub. As is frequently done in Scripture, the devil is addressed through a man of earth—in this instance, the king of Tyre. But the passage can refer to none other than Satan himself:

Son of man, take up a lamentation upon the king of Tyrus, and say unto him, Thus saith the Lord God; Thou sealest up the sum, full of wisdom, and perfect in beauty. Thou hast been in Eden the garden of God; every precious stone was thy covering, the sardius, topaz, and the diamond, the beryl, the onyx, and the jasper, the sapphire, the emerald, and the carbuncle, and gold: the workmanship of thy tabrets and of thy pipes was prepared in thee in the day that thou wast created. Thou art the anointed cherub that covereth; and I have set thee so: thou wast upon the holy mountain of God; thou hast walked up and down in the midst of the stones of fire. Thou wast perfect in thy ways from the day that thou wast created, till iniquity was found in thee.

Ezekiel 28:12–15

No king of Tyre has ever been in either the earthly Eden or that Eden mentioned in this passage. The reference is, therefore, to someone else, someone who once enjoyed a celestial habitat with supernatural glory. And that person was Lucifer.

It is important that we note the statement, "Thou wast perfect in thy ways from the day that thou wast created, till *iniquity* was found in thee." In this study, it is important that we understand that Lucifer was created, and does not exist in and of himself. There has always been a human tendency to believe that two powers exist, one good and one evil, and that the two are equal. According to this erroneous concept, God is accepted as the ruler of the good, and Satan of the evil. While it is indeed true that two powers exist—one good and one evil; one of God and one of Satan—it is by no means true that they are equal: *Satan was created; God is the Creator.*

God did not create Satan as a force of evil, but as Lucifer, Son of the Morning, perfect in beauty, full of wisdom, "the anointed cherub that covereth." And the cherub remained in the state of perfection until iniquity was born in him, and an unprecedented evil arose in his heart. Thus, through iniquity, he became Satan—the deceiver, the father of lies, the source of all evil.

The Birth of Iniquity

The presumption and arrogance that brought about the fall of Lucifer stagger the imagination of Christian men.

Somehow it entered the mind of the creature that he could become equal to the Creator! He did not propose to become merely a fiend or a devil ... simply to fall from his place in heaven. On the contrary, he intended to be like God, and to climb above Him in the heavenly sphere.

Isaiah 14:12–15 details the iniquity of Lucifer, and the towering presumptions of his heart:

> How art thou fallen from heaven, O Lucifer, son of the morning! how art thou cut down to the ground, which didst weaken the nations! For thou hast said in thine heart, I will ascend into heaven, I will exalt my throne above the stars of God: I will sit also upon the mount of the congregation, in the sides of the north: I will ascend above the heights of the clouds; I will be like the most High. Yet thou shalt be brought down to hell, to the sides of the pit.

The five-fold platform of rebellion is clear in its aims: the creature actually proposed to overthrow and take the place of his Creator. He reached this insane presumption through pride in his wisdom and beauty, forgetting that these were the work of the Creator. In *Paradise Lost,* John Milton posits that the catalyst for Lucifer's iniquity was jealousy over the preeminence of Christ as God's son. But that is poetry; there is no theological answer to the eternal question of why Lucifer did it. We can, however, review the stated aims of his rebellion that gave birth to iniquity in the universe:

"I will ascend into heaven." The purpose stated here was to invade the very precincts of heaven where the throne of God is. Lucifer dared aspire to a domain reserved for deity. That there are levels or stages in heaven is intimated in Paul's testimony that he had, either in a vision or in his body, been "caught up to the third heaven" (2 Corinthians 12:2). It is generally accepted that the earth's atmosphere is the first heaven, the starry universe the second, and the abode of God the third. From an analysis of the further goals stated by Lucifer, we know that his ambition was to occupy the place

of God. He who had been created by the hand of God now assumed to move God off His throne and to usurp His authority. He who was created full of wisdom, by iniquity became filled with evil folly.

"I will exalt my throne above the stars of God." The vaunted ambition of Lucifer included lordship over the creation of God. This point in the rebellious program is an explicit reference to divine sovereignty and rulership, to the very throne from which God rules creation. The host of heaven was sometimes referred to as the stars of God (Job 38:7), and the word *star* is frequently used as a figurative reference to Christ and His Church (Numbers 24:7; Revelation 1:16, 20). "I Jesus have sent mine angel to testify unto you these things in the churches. I am the root and the offspring of David, and the bright and morning star" (Revelation 22:16). The intention of Lucifer, therefore, was to assert supremacy over the celestial creation of God.

"I will sit upon the mount of the congregation in the sides of the north." The ambition of Satan centered in a desire to rule the universe and gain its worship. This aspect of his scheme emphasizes his intention to control the world's religion. The word *mount* suggests rulership, and *congregation* connotes worship (Isaiah 2:2; Psalms 48:2). In the Psalms reference, Jerusalem—the spiritual center of Jewish and Chritian faith—is spoken of in language similar to that used by Satan. "Beautiful for situation, the joy of the whole earth, is mount Zion, on the sides of the north, the city of the great King" (Psalms 48:2). His goal was clear: he would rule the universe and all creation would worship him.

"I will ascend above the heights of the clouds." From the earliest times, clouds have been associated with the glory of God. During the wilderness journeys of the Israelites, it was an accompanying cloud that represented the guiding presence of God: "Behold, the glory of the Lord appeared in the cloud" (Exodus 16:10). Throughout the wilderness experience, God

manifested Himself in clouds, as when the tabernacle was completed: "Then," it is written, "a cloud covered the tent of the congregation, and the glory of the Lord filled the tabernacle" (Exodus 40:34). A cloud continued to represent the visible evidence of God's presence, as when Solomon completed his great temple of the Lord. At that time, "The cloud filled the house of the Lord," and "the glory of the Lord had filled the house of the Lord" (1 Kings 8:10, 11). At His Second Coming, Christ will be revealed "in the clouds of heaven with power and great glory" (Matthew 24:30).

What Lucifer set out to do now becomes quite clear—he would establish for himself a glory surpassing that of God Himself. This arrogance is so preposterous that it defies comprehension—yet it happened! Lucifer became intent upon displacing and exceeding God, whose authority and glory filled all the universe.

"I will be like the most high." At last Lucifer enunciated the heart of his evil design by placing himself in direct comparison with God. He had mentioned heaven, the stars of God, His holy mount, the clouds of His glory—but now he stated his intentions toward God Himself: Lucifer would be like Him. He who had been the highest of God's creation, the wisest and most beautiful, now aspired to be higher still. He was wise, but he wanted to be omniscient, to know all things; he was powerful, but he wanted to be omnipotent, to be all-powerful; he was capable of going anywhere in the universe, but he wanted to be omnipresent, to be everywhere. In short, Satan wanted no authority, no presence, and no glory above his own.

Even today, Satan's declaration of intent boggles the mind with its presumption, its arrogance, its devilish insanity. Yet, insane and inconceivable as it is, it was Lucifer's original purpose, and, as we shall see later, it has not been abandoned or significantly altered to this day. He *still* would be like the Most High. He *still* intends to take the place of God.

Desire for Omnipotence

Satan's program of usurpation stemmed from his desire for omnipotence. If he could only attain that goal, he would be unequalled in the universe, for it is impossible to divide omnipotence. If two things are equally powerful, neither can be said to be all-powerful, for neither has power over the other: Two equal powers cancel each other. Omnipotence must stand alone—and only God is omnipotent.

Satan's ambition to be like God, therefore, was not a desire to share divine dominion, but to supplant it. Having developed an intense jealousy of his Creator, he undertook to replace Him as sovereign over all creation. In Ezekiel 28, we see the extent of that mad presumption. There—and we must still be mindful of the device of speaking to Satan through the prince of Tyre—we twice read the words, "thou [hast] set thine heart as the heart of God" (verses 2, 6). The devil's craving for omnipotence is seen as a progressive delusion, from the comparative "I am a god" and "I sit in the seat of God" (verse 2) to the absolute "I am God" (verse 9).

His intention was total delusion: there was never a moment of time when Lucifer's plan had the slightest possibility of success. Such an ambition as his is so preposterous that one might discard it as mockery or fable if history did not so frequently ring with its echo—an echo heard in the lives of mortals in almost every generation. We heard it first in the Garden of Eden when the tempter beguiled Adam and Eve with the possibility of being as gods (Genesis 3:5) We heard it in the tones of the morbid religions practiced by mankind when Egyptian Pharaohs were worshipped as gods, as were the Babylonian kings, the Roman Caesars, and many others.

The devil tempted Jesus to bow down and worship him (Matthew 4:9), and he will set up worship of himself in the last days (Revelation 13:12–15). He has not given up his lust for omnipotence, and for the glory and worship it will bring. His idea is echoed in the widespread satanism and cultic worship of our day, which, as we shall see, become increasingly overt in practice and satanic in purpose.

Lucifer conceived his platform aeons ago and has pressed it assiduously ever since. Through the ages he has alternated between aggressiveness and stealth, according to the mood and circumstance of the time; but now, as we near the endtime, he is becoming more and more open about his aims—and more and more determined in their pursuit. The result is a new surge of demonic power that will be pressed ever more ruthlessly as time passes, and with it a revival of devilish beliefs that will be pushed more determinedly than ever before.

> If he were beautiful
> As he is hideous now, and yet did dare
> To scowl upon his Maker, well from him
> May all our misery flow.
>
> Dante
> *The Divine Comedy*

4
Satan, the Adversary

When Hitler came to power in Germany he had no intention of becoming a villain—a symbol of primitive evil in a civilized world. Instead, he viewed himself as a great champion, a leader to be admired and adored by the Aryan people of earth. His twisted mind was so perverted that he saw his malevolent cause as proper and good. It has been the same with other great villains of earth, right down to Stalin and Idi Amin, who follow the pattern of the one who inspired them, the devil. No monster ever announces, "I'll become a monster." He starts out with something else—something more high-sounding—in mind.

Lucifer, too, did not set out to become a fiend, but a god. He did not intend to be a devil, but like the Most High. He did not want to be lord of the underworld (as mortal concepts now sometimes depict him), but the omnipotent sovereign of the universe. But thwarted in his scheme to be God, he became a devil, the father of all evil.

Satan's Fall

The word *devil* is a shortened form of the Greek word *diabolos,* which means an accuser or deceiver. This fits well, for Lucifer's career, since his fall, has been one of malicious deceit and evil. The rebellion of Lucifer subverted a large portion of the angelic host, because he was an angel of the highest order, with other angels under his influence. Although there is no detailed record of what happened, we get some idea from Revelation 12:9 of the chaos created by that rebellion:

And the great dragon was cast out, that old serpent, called the Devil, and Satan, which deceiveth the whole world: he was cast out into the earth, and his angels were cast out with him.

In Revelation 12:4, we read that a third of the heavenly host fell with Satan. Their fall was a direct consequence of the devil's influence: "his tail drew the third part of the stars of heaven, and did cast them to the earth. . . ." The word *stars* in this verse clearly refers to angels.

The term *his angels* used in verses 7 and 9 indicates the power and authority Satan enjoyed in the ages prior to his revolt against God. The fact that Michael and his angels are also mentioned in verse 7 indicates the exalted position of the two archangels in the universe before the creation of man. The angelic eminence of Michael is also mentioned in Daniel 12:1, where he is referred to as "the great prince which standeth for the children of thy people." (The reference is to Michael's particular relationship to Israel.) From the time of Lucifer's rebellion, he has been opposed by the faithful champion of God, Michael.

The Demonic Horde

What of the angels that fell with Lucifer? Just as he became Diabolos, the adversary, so his angels became the demons that yet remain obedient to him and ready to do his bidding. Matthew 25:41, which reveals the ultimate doom of Satan and his demonic horde, refers to them again as "his angels." Such clues are important, for they confirm that the angels that followed Lucifer in his primordial revolt are today the demons that maintain allegiance to him, serve his purposes, and represent his cause in the world. Satan does not share God's omnipresence any more than he does His omnipotence, but his demon agents are able to represent him in all places.

There is a great, perhaps countless, host of demons afoot in the world. The Scripture gives no clue regarding the number; we know only that they once constituted a third of the heavenly host. In any event, the demonic horde is vast enough to convince the unknowing that Satan's power is virtually equal to God's. But, as we shall see later, that is not true by any means. Satan is but a creature, wise and cunning as he may be, in competition with the Creator for the allegiance of man. He must rely upon his *ability to deceive* in order to achieve his ends. We don't know what ruse he used to deceive his angels into following him (although we may guess that it was pride, desire for position and power, jealousy and the like); but we do know of his deceptions of man, which are called devices and wiles (2 Corinthians 2:11; Ephesians 6:11).

Satan on Earth

Thwarted in his attempt to rule the universe, Satan was cast out of heaven (Luke 10:18) and became the prince of the power of the air (Ephesians 2:2). It was probably at this time that the earth became without form and void (Genesis 1:2). Satan began his deceptive campaign against God's earthly creation almost immediately. When Adam and Eve were in the Garden of Eden, both themselves and the garden itself in a state of creative perfection (Genesis 2:7-15), Satan, with all cunning and guile, appeared to them in the form of a serpent. His campaign against them—the same he wages with men today—was a devilish mixture of truth and falsehood, fact and innuendo. (The devil seldom deals with total lies, for they are too easily discerned by the wise. He much prefers to approach man with half-truths that contain the seeds of destruction.)

We do not know how long Satan tempted and taunted Adam and Eve before they yielded to him, though the early Jewish fathers believed it to be about 150 years. Persistence is one of Satan's strong points—he never really gives up. Even at the end of this age, he will still hold to the horrible scheme that made him the devil.

When Adam and Eve yielded to the serpent's wiles by eating the forbidden fruit (Genesis 3:1–6), they seemed to have been most influenced by his suggestion that it would make them godlike, wise, and knowing. They learned quickly that they had been deceived, when they came to know evil by experience and guilt, rather than by superior knowledge (verse 7). Their sin of disobedience was a triumph for the devil, for with it sin passed into the human race and made all men subject to death (Romans 5:12). Now, instead of direct fellowship, it would hereafter require a mediator to reconcile God and man—and such reconciliation would be on an individual basis. Each person would have to make his own commitment to God. The Mediator is, of course, Jesus Christ, and our individual acceptance of Him is that act of personal commitment that unites us with God the Father.

The great objective of the devil is to prevent this union of God and man, and to establish himself as the lord of earth. He is, therefore, the accuser and adversary of man as well as of God. He accuses each to the other, and exerts every effort to keep them estranged. When a man does not accept the atonement provided by Christ, he provides the devil with a certain spiritual victory. He does not have to do more.

The Accuser

Christians especially are opposed by the devil, who would effect their downfall. "Be sober, be vigilant; because your adversary the devil, as a roaring lion, walketh about, seeking whom he may devour" (1 Peter 5:8). In the story of Job we have a picture of the devil at work. When the sons of God (angels) made an appearance before the Lord, Satan appeared with them (Job 1). Upon being questioned about his origins, Satan replied, "From going to and fro in the earth, and from walking up and down in it" (verse 7). The inference was that the earth and its people belonged to him—that he had been afoot in his domain like a landlord surveying his estate.

Satan was contemptuous, filled with arrogance and accusation. It is for that reason that God cited Job to him, calling Job "a perfect and an upright man, one that feareth God, and escheweth evil" (verse 8). The trials and triumph of Job are well-known; our point here is to note Satan's presumption that all the world is his.

This presumption was repeated more overtly when he confronted Jesus on the mount of temptation:

> Again, the devil taketh him up into an exceeding high mountain, and sheweth him all the kingdoms of the world, and the glory of them; And saith unto him, All these things will I give thee, if thou wilt fall down and worship me.
>
> Matthew 4:8, 9

Clearly, the devil presumed the world to be his domain, for him to use as he would. He regarded himself as ruler and sovereign of the earth. There is ample scriptural evidence of Satan's referring to himself as a prince or god:

Prince of the devils (Matthew 12:24).
Prince of this world (John 12:31).
Prince of this world (John 14:30).
Prince of this world (John 16:11).
Prince of the powers of the air (Ephesians 2:2).
God of this world (2 Corinthians 4:4).

The royal titles reflect both the exalted position he once held and the tremendous influence he still holds in the world. Except for the restraining power of the Holy Spirit (2 Thessalonians 2:7) and the resistance of the saints of God (Ephesians 6:10–18; James 4:7; 1 Peter 5:8–10), Satan would gain unquestioned supremacy over the world. But those restraining forces are present to frustrate the accomplishment of his goals, and may God be praised for that. While worldly men are easy prey for the devil, the child of God is not subject to him (2 Timothy 2:26).

Satan's Influence

The extent of Satan's influence in the world today can scarcely be overstated. We see it in innumerable ways, from out-and-out paganism, in heathen and civilized lands alike; in brutal and inhuman behavior by his followers; to super-stitious admixtures of worship and craven fear by those who confess the name of Christ.

It is important for Christians to know what power the devil has, and equally important to know the limits of that power. Satan is well served when we underestimate him, for we then let down our defenses against him. He is equally well served when an overestimation of him fills our lives with fear and dread. If the devil cannot make men doubt his exis-tence and therefore be unwary of his devices, then he would have them become so frightened of him that he can control them through fear. The devil has power, true enough, but by no means all power; he is wise, but not all-wise; he moves freely in the universe, but he cannot be everywhere at the same time. *Only God is omnipotent, omniscient, and omnipresent.*

In our generation, we have seen the entire gamut of no-tions about the devil, from sophisticated disbelief to ob-sessive fascination. Motion pictures such as *The Exorcist, The Omen, The Demons, The Legions of Lucifer, Rosemary's Baby, Da-mien,* and so on have made a fetish of demon influence and possession. Publishers rival this motion-picture preoccupa-tion with such books as *The Possession of Joel Delaney* and *The Other,* and such manual-type offerings as *The Book of Shadows, The Satanic Bible,* and *The Compleat Witch.* Having been brought out into the open, the devil now seems intent upon saturating the world with a more or less confused awareness of his presence. As *Newsweek* magazine said in the course of reviewing the plethora of recent movies on satanic themes, "Though Hollywood has yet to disgorge a born-again epic, it has massaged Christianity's black underside to death. . . ." Much of the garble is exaggeration and diversion, while the devil works undisturbed to achieve his real aims.

Demonism is a very real possibility today. There are powers abroad that afflict the human body and mind, just as there were in Bible days. And there are demons that work perversity and violence when those conditions fit the designs of Satan. I am convinced, however, that these evils are not the proudest products of the devil, but only by-products of his chief aim: the usurpation of worship and allegiance that belong to God. All forms of evil stem from that intention, just as evil itself began with Satan's ambition to be like God.

PART II
The Pattern of Apostasy

5

A Religious Devil

Satan is consistently, emphatically religious. Not Christian, mind you, not holy—but religious. He became the devil by trying to become like God. But, although he declared his intention to attain the throne of God, he nowhere mentioned a desire for the holiness or nature of God. The two desires would have been mutually exclusive—and Satan wanted power. Cast out of heaven for his rebellion, the devil intensified his efforts on earth; he simply revised his strategy, not his aims. And his new strategy had to involve man as well as God, because of those unique qualities God had given man.

When God created man, He made him in His own image (Genesis 1:27), which, for one thing, means that man was endowed with some of God's own attributes—not the least of which was will. One manifest reason for this was that God wished to enjoy fellowship with man. Other earthly creatures—beasts, birds, fish—lacking the gift of will, followed their creature instinct: their obedience to God's laws was not a matter of volition, but the involuntary following of nature. Man, however, was altogether different: his obedience and worship would be a matter of choice. But obedience is proved by the possibility of disobedience, for which reason God placed a tree in the garden, whose fruit Adam and Eve were forbidden to eat.

Satan's Strategy of Separation

As long as God and man enjoyed Creator–creature fellowship there was no place for Satan. It therefore became essential to the aims of Satan to drive a wedge between God and man. We see his vile footprint in the garden when, as a serpent, he vilified God by suggesting to Adam that God was both untruthful and insincere in dealing with His creature. He insisted that God lied when He said death would result from eating the forbidden fruit: such was not the case, they would not "surely die" (Genesis 3:3, 4). And God, according to Satan, was insincere: He really wished them to abstain from the fruit because it would bring them the benefit of *being like gods,* knowledgeable and wise (3:5). The strategem worked: Adam and Eve partook of the fruit, and lost their innocent fellowship with God.

The success of Satan's scheme disrupted the simple communion of God and man, and necessitated a more formal vehicle of fellowship between them. The two would inevitably grow farther apart with the passing of time, which would allow Satan further to confuse and distort man's comprehension of God. When God introduced a formal religion whereby man could worship Him, Satan initiated a myriad of false religions that served his foul purposes.

Multiple Gods

Satan, as stated previously, is basically and thoroughly religious. He wanted—and wants—to be God, or even *a* god, claiming the worship of the universe. Under his deceitful influence, man's inherent need to worship God was perverted to the worship of false gods, or, more appropriately, man's devotion was turned to the devil (hiding behind many guises and names). Men who forgot the true God became entangled in perverted and horrible practices of worship:

Because that, when they knew God, they glorified him not as God, neither were thankful; but became vain in their imaginations, and their foolish heart was darkened. Professing themselves to be wise, they became fools, And changed the glory of the uncorruptible God into an image made like to corruptible man, and to birds, and fourfooted beasts, and creeping things.

Romans 1:21–23

Religion flourished in the ancient world—practically all of it apostate. A devil-inspired religion, devised to satisfy whatever the morbid nature of man might desire. Except for the true faith of God held by the children of Abraham, the world became filled with apostasy. As it is said in Scripture: "Certain men, the children of Belial, are gone out from among you, and have withdrawn the inhabitants of their city, saying, Let us go and serve other gods, which ye have not known" (Deuteronomy 13:13). In the Old Testament, Satan was frequently referred to as Belial—a profane or worthless one—and those who did not worship God in truth were called children of Belial (Deuteronomy 13:13; Judges 19:22; 1 Samuel 10:27; 25:25).

The devil does not discourage worship; he would only pervert it with lies and deception, thereby turning it to himself. The poet Milton captures this truth very well:

> By falsities and lies the greatest part
> Of Mankind they corrupted to forsake
> God their Creator, and the invisible
> Glory of him that made them to transform
> Oft to the image of a brute, adorned
> With gay religions full of pomp and gold,
> And devils to adore for deities.
>
> John Milton
> *Paradise Lost*

Men came to worship many things, such as the sun, the sky, the moon, fire, water, vegetation, and almost every natural feature of the earth. To these were added many of earth's creatures, such as the bull, the crocodile, the monkey, the falcon, the cat, the cow, the jackal, the wolf, the eagle, and—above all—the serpent. Among the mightiest of the deities were the leaders of the nations: the Pharaohs of

Egypt; the kings of Babylon, Assyria, and other nations; the Caesars of Rome; and the chiefs of lesser people and tribes. To the people, these emperor-gods were all-powerful. With a gesture, they could give life; with the opposite gesture, cause a man to die; with the wave of a wand, send forth thousands to fight and die.

In addition to these deities he could see, man invented a multitude of invisible gods that reflected his fertile imagination and the deepest longings of his God-given nature. The nations adjoining Israel, for example, were saturated with idolatry. Egypt had literally hundreds of deities, with names like Horus, Osiris, Amon, Aton, Ptah, Ra, and Isis. Babylon's pantheon of gods equalled Egypt's, with deities called Ishtar, Sin, Marduk, and Ninmah. Virtually all the gods were identified jealously with one or another nation, with no power or authority beyond the borders of the land where they were worshipped.

Apostate Israel

In the midst of the religious confusion was Israel, where the worship of Jehovah was preserved. Their worship of Jehovah, and only Jehovah, is what made Israel a special people. The devil repeatedly and persistently introduced other worship forms into the land, thereby to contaminate the pure worship of God. When true worship is defiled, the worship of Satan is enhanced.

Early in the biblical record, we encounter the false religions of the devil. Even as the Israelites fled from slavery in Egypt, they were inclined to worship the gods of Egypt. The people demanded of Aaron, "Up, make us gods, which shall go before us . . ." (Exodus 32:1). The bull-god, Apis, sacred to the Egyptians, was the model for a calf of gold which the newly freed Hebrews worshipped. When Moses left them to spend a period upon the sacred mountain, the people were left fearful and alone. They needed some object they could see and feel—something for the here and now. Taking advantage of their confused emotions, Satan reminded them of their past life in Egypt, where their masters had seemed powerful and secure. Thus, the lonely Hebrews were drawn to an object that represented security and satisfaction—the sacred bull-god of Egypt. And they demanded that Aaron make a calf of gold for them, and gladly delivered up their gold for its construction.

So the pattern of apostasy was acted out to the end. The people needed to worship, and worship they did. They needed something they could see and feel—something they could associate with Egyptian power and provision . . . something to remind them of their familiar past. Furthermore, they needed a touch of mysticism and wonder, all of which the calf or bull, Apis, represented to them. There was also a sexual imagery in the procreative energies of the bull, which inspired sexual license in its presence; so they fell down before it, and danced and cavorted in sensual orgiastic worship. Under the prodding of Satan, they could experience awe, excitement, and release in the orgy of worship. To them, Jehovah seemed far away, but Apis the bull was here and now. Jehovah was a father-image who terrified disobedient children, but Apis was license and gratification. While the Hebrews cavorted before the calf, Satan must have been somewhere nearby, chortling with glee.

That is the way of apostasy. Satan plays upon man's urge to worship, but he corrupts the true worship of God by injecting all sorts of ungodly elements into its practice. He thereby spoils the worship of God, and perverts it to himself. Again and again in the checkered spiritual history of Israel, the Jews vacillated between God and the array of false gods Satan paraded before them.

In the end, it would be Israel's worship of the gods of Canaan that would cause their downfall. The ten northern tribes, taken captive by Assyria 150 years before the fall of Judah, lost their souls and their homeland because they adopted the heathen practices of Canaan. "They built them high places in all their cities ... and ... set them up images and groves in every high hill, and under every green tree: And there they burnt incense in all the high places, as did the heathen whom the Lord carried away before them ..." (2 Kings 17:9–11).

They were lost as a people because of the very sins that had earlier destroyed the people of Canaan:

> And they left all the commandments of the Lord their God, and made them molten images, even two calves, and made a grove, and worshipped all the host of heaven, and served Baal. And they caused their sons and their daughters to pass through the fire, and used divination and enchantments, and sold themselves to do evil in the sight of the Lord, to provoke him to anger. Therefore the Lord was very angry with Israel, and removed them out of his sight: there was none left but the tribe of Judah only.
>
> 2 Kings 17:16–18

Baal. Baal (plural Baalim) was a god of the Canaanites. The Baalim or Baals were worshipped throughout Palestine at the time the Hebrews entered the land, and these local deities were the most successful apostate device used by the devil in the early history of Israel. The gods were worshipped in nature—outdoors, on hilltops, in forest groves (Deuteronomy 12:2, 3; Judges 6:25; 1 Kings 16:31–33). The worship of Baal was so deep-rooted in the land that it proved to be a lasting confusion to Israel. Although various Jewish leaders attempted to stamp it out, worship of Baal endured for many years.

Among those who opposed it were Gideon (Judges 6:25), Jehu (2 Kings 10:18), Jehoiada (2 Kings 11:17), and Josiah (2 Kings 23:4). The most dramatic effort to extirpate Baalism was Elijah's encounter with the priests of Baal on Mount Carmel (1 Kings 18:18–40), when, under the influence of the infamous Jezebel, worship of Baal had virtually replaced worship of Jehovah. Jezebel, a native Zidonian princess, had grown up worshipping Baal, and when she married Ahab, king of Israel, Baalism was installed as the *de facto* state religion in Samaria. That was a real coup for the devil, and only a person of Elijah's zeal and courage would have dared challenge it as he did. The prophet's challenge to 850 prophets of Baal; his derision of their misguided zeal; his bold extension of the odds against his own success by drenching the sacrifice with water; his dramatic call for fire from heaven; and, finally, his execution of the false prophets—together constitute one of the most heroic stories of the Old Testament.

Ashtoreth. The goddess Ashtoreth, a Canaanite deity worshipped widely along the coasts of Palestine, was a goddess of fertility, worshipped with lewd sexual rites. According to Judges 2:12, 13, the Hebrews "forsook the Lord ... and served Baal and Ashtoreth." Both Baal and Ashtoreth were "worshipped" with licentious sexual acts in the groves and high places. During his lifetime, Samuel influenced the people to return to God, abandoning the worship of Baalim and Ashtoreth (1 Samuel 7:3, 4).

Dagon. Another god the Jews were acquainted with was Dagon, chief deity of the Philistines—although the Jews did not serve him widely. Place names in Judah and Asher bore Dagon's name (Joshua 15:41; 19:27). It was his temple that Samson destroyed (Judges 16:23, 30), and it was the image of Dagon that collapsed in the presence of the ark of God (1 Samuel 5:1-4). Saul's head was displayed in the temple of Dagon following his defeat by the Philistines (1 Chronicles 10:10). It must have given the devil great satisfaction that two of God's champions should end up in a temple of the fish-god.

Molech. When Satan introduced Israel to the Ammonite god Molech, he demonstrated the lowest side of his cruel nature: Molech was worshipped by human sacrifice, especially the sacrifice of children. The Jewish allegiance to Jehovah sank to a pitiful low when the Jews put their own children to death in search of a false deity's acceptance.

Before the Israelites entered Canaan, God had specifically warned them against the horrible worship of Molech.

Again, thou shalt say to the children of Israel, Whosoever he be of the children of Israel, or of the strangers that sojourn in Israel, that giveth any of his seed unto Molech; he shall surely be put to death: the people of the land shall stone him with stones. And I will set my face against that man, and will cut him off from among his people; because he hath given of his seed unto Molech, to defile my sanctuary, and to profane my holy name. And if the people of the land do any ways hide their eyes from the man, when he giveth of his seed unto Molech, and kill him not: then I will set my face against that man, and against his family, and will cut him off, and all that go a whoring after him, to commit whoredom with Molech, from among their people.

Leviticus 20:2–5

Huge images of Molech (or Moloch, Malcam, or Milcom, as he was variously called) were erected in Israel. His arms were used as fiery altars, where the slaughtered children were burned in sacrifice to propitiate the anger—or satisfy the hunger—of the god. Tragically, the Jews tried to blend their devotion to God and Molech by going from one place of worship to the other—an iniquitous practice decried by both Ezekiel and Jeremiah.

That they have committed adultery, and blood is in their hands, and with their idols have they committed adultery, and have also caused their sons, whom they bare unto me, to pass for them through the fire, to devour them. Moreover this they have done unto me: they have defiled my sanctuary in the same day, and have profaned my sabbaths. For when they had slain their children to their idols, then they came the same day into my sanctuary to profane it; and, lo, thus have they done in the midst of mine house.

Ezekiel 23:37–39

Will ye steal, murder, and commit adultery, and swear falsely, and burn incense unto Baal, and walk after other gods whom ye know not; And come and stand before me in this house, which is called by my name, and say, We are delivered to do all these abominations?

Jeremiah 7:9, 10

Because they have forsaken me, and have estranged this place, and have burned incense in it unto other gods, whom neither they nor their fathers have known, nor the kings of Judah, and have filled this place with the blood of innocents; They have built also the high places of Baal, to burn their sons with fire for burnt offerings unto Baal, which I commanded not, nor spake *it,* neither came *it* into my mind.

Jeremiah 19:4, 5

The worship of God became so perverted that the Jews hardly knew whom they worshipped, or how. The word *hell* stems from the depressing idolatry in Judah. A popular place of pagan sacrifice was the valley of Hinnom, from which comes the word *Gehenna,* which in turn is the root word for *hell* (Jeremiah 19:6). The devil never discourages religion: he promotes it, and twists it to serve himself.

The Apostate King

One of the most bewildering cases of apostasy in Israel's history is that of King Solomon. He who began his reign with a humble appeal to God for sufficient wisdom to lead his people in truth (1 Kings 3:9), and who lifted the moral tone of the nation with his prayer at the dedication of his great temple (1 Kings 8:22–53), in the end demonstrated the grossest pride and sank the nation's spiritual plane to an apostate level. In a way, his diplomatic success caused his spiritual downfall! In the course of military victories and diplomatic adventures, Solomon formed an unbelievable number of state alliances, sealed by marriage to noble princesses. These eventually numbered seven hundred wives and three hundred concubines (1 Kings 11:1–3), but the domestic chaos created by such a formidable circumstance was nothing to compare with the spiritual consequences it had.

The Song of Solomon shows the king to have been a romantically sensitive man—a characteristic that inclined him to accommodate his wives' whims and desires. Moreover, it was very likely a condition of the marriage compacts that there would be no interference with his wives' religion. But whatever the background, the situation resulted in Solomon's undoing. He not only did not interfere with, but made provisions for, his wives' pagan worship. He might better have attempted to win them to the true faith of Jehovah.

The once wise and devoted king was, also, prey to the purpose of the devil. He who first tolerated the false worship of his wives came, in time, to join them in the worship:

> For it came to pass, when Solomon was old, that his wives turned away his heart after other gods. . . . For Solomon went after Ashtoreth the goddess of the Zidonians, and after Milcom the abomination of the Ammonites. . . . Then did Solomon build an high place for Chemosh, the abomination of Moab, in the hill that is before Jerusalem, and for Molech, the abomination of the children of Ammon. And likewise did he for all his strange wives, which burnt incense and sacrificed unto their gods.
>
> 1 Kings 11:4–8

Satan did his work successfully. He brought about the downfall of a man and the apostasy of a people not by denying religion, but by perverting it. He did not oppose God's temple in Jerusalem—he merely added to it a temple of vice for Ashtoreth, a temple of rioting for Chemosh, and altars of human sacrifice for Molech and Milcom.

That was, and still is, the strategy of Satan and the pattern of apostasy.

6

Sanctuaries of Satan

If the devil were antireligious, or even nonreligious, the world would have been atheistic—without any religion—when Jesus was born. For, except for the Judean oasis, the world was under Satan's undisputed influence at that time. The devil was enjoying his period of greatest success, with no righteous influence, such as the Church of today, dedicated to restraining him. He held the world in his lap, able to make of it what he would—and yet, rather than nonreligious, the world has seldom been more completely religious! But it was a pagan world (except for the Jewish worship of God), with thousands of deities to claim the fearful, ignorant, adoring worship of man. The world, like Athens, was "wholly given to idolatry" (Acts 17:16).

There are no limits to the breadth of Satan's distortion of man's inherent need to worship. He takes advantage of man's yearning for fellowship with God, and perverts it into something false and ugly . . . something morbid and violent.

The Pagan World

Under Satan's dominion, the pre-Christian earth had become filled with religion—with gods, demons, witches, and sorcerers, and perverted worship of every sort. The gods mentioned in the Old Testament had largely been exchanged for new gods in more distant parts of the world. And the highly civilized character of some of the peoples of the earth in no way diminished their belief in pagan gods: Greece, its admirable Hellenic culture notwithstanding, was thrall to a pantheon of deities—Zeus, the supreme god; Hera, his wife; Poseidon, god of the sea; Athena, goddess of wisdom; and literally hundreds of others.

Rome, which occupied Israel during the lifetime of Jesus, had its own variations of every known deity, which the Romans worshipped throughout their empire: Jupiter, the prime god; Mars, god of war; Quirinus, the state god; Apollo, god of literature and healing; Mercury, messenger of the gods; and an elaborate array of others, applicable to every human circumstance. Among the goddesses were Juno, wife of Jupiter; Vesta, the hearth-goddess; Ceres, goddess of grain; and—above all—Cybele, mother of the gods.

Understandably, the deities of love—the prevalence of which emphasizes man's timeless need of love—were popular in every nation and culture. The gods Eros and Cupid, along with the goddesses Aphrodite, Venus, Artemis, Isis, and Diana, represented the deep longings of man in many lands, and gave a hollow focus to his needs. Similarly, such gods as Dionysus and Bacchus spoke with wine and revelry of man's need to forget his misery and longings.

It is interesting to note that Barnabas and Paul were mistaken for Jupiter and Mercury in Lystra of Asia Minor:

And when the people saw what Paul had done, they lifted up their voices, saying in the speech of Lycaonia, The gods are come down to us in the likeness of men. And they called Barnabas, Jupiter; and Paul, Mercurius, because he was the chief speaker. Then the priest of Jupiter, which was before their city, brought oxen and garlands unto the gates, and would have done sacrifice with the people. Which when the apostles, Barnabas and Paul, heard of, they rent their clothes, and ran in among the people, crying out, and saying, Sirs, why do ye these things? We also are men of like passions with you, and preach unto you that ye should turn from these vanities unto the living God, which made heaven, and earth, and the sea, and all things that are therein.

Acts 14:11–15

At the time of this incident, Barnabas, the elder evangelist, was taken to be Jupiter, while Paul, the spokesman for the pair, was taken to be Mercury. The priest of Jupiter either believed as the people did or took advantage of the people's superstition, and undertook to worship the two apostles. Barnabas and Paul, for their part, took advantage of the ensuing confusion to preach to the people. But even with their denials that they were gods, the apostles had a difficult time preventing the sacrifice in their honor (Acts 14:18).

At a later time Paul, as he was being taken to Rome under arrest, was taken to be a god. On the island of Melita he was bitten by a snake, which he shook off his hand without harm (Acts 28:1–6). The superstitious witnesses of the event at first reasoned that Paul was a murderer, and that some retributive force (using the serpent as its instrument) had tracked him down. When no harm came to Paul, the pendulum of superstition swung to the opposite extreme: The Melitans concluded that he was a god.

Thus deeply was man committed to the worship of his gods. So thoroughly had the devil perverted man's need to worship God. So widely had he spread his sanctuaries in the world.

A Savage Faith

Unrestrained, the religions of Satan were more than morbid—they were macabre, brutal, and tragic, before the coming of the Messiah. The era of Christ and the apostles was also dominated by devilish religions, with barbarities that belied the advanced knowledge of the day. The people of that time accepted the necessity of human sacrifice to propitiate the hordes of gods and demon spirits that populated the world. They believed that vengeful deities had to be gratified with human flesh or provided with human companionship. The result was universal human sacrifice on a scale no less brutal than it had been earlier among Israel's neighbors.

Edward Westermarck observed, in *The Origin and Development of Moral Ideas:*

Men are killed with a view to gratifying the desires of superhuman beings. We meet with human sacrifice in the past history of every so-called Aryan race. There are numerous indications that it was known among the early Greeks. At certain times it prevailed in the Hellenic cult of Zeus; indeed, in the second century after Christ men seem still to have been sacrificed to Zeus Lycaeus in Arcadia....

In Rome, also, human sacrifices, though exceptional, were not unknown in historical times.... Tertullian states that in North Africa, even to the proconsulship of Tiberius, infants were publicly sacrificed to Saturn.

The ritualistic killing was not confined to savage races; on the contrary, it was more frequently found among barbarians and semi-civilized peoples than among genuine savages. Satan had the world going his way until the intrusion of the Christian message into that world—for it was to heathen lands where such digressions of worship existed that the apostles carried Christ's message of love.

The macabre rite of killing humans to propitiate gods continued in many parts of the world until fairly recent times, or until such time as the races that so appeased their deities were reached by the Gospel of Christ. According to Prescott's *History of the Conquest of Mexico,* the Western Hemisphere was the scene of prodigious religious killings. He speaks of annual sacrifices of twenty thousand victims, and more. (Some historians place the number at an appalling seventy thousand human lives a year!) It is said that fourteen thousand humans were sacrificed at the dedication of the Aztec shrine to the feathered-serpent god, Quetzalcoatl, in Teotihuacan. Prescott also records:

At the dedication of the great temple of Huitzilopotchli, in 1486, the prisoners, who for some years had been reserved for the purpose, were drawn from all quarters to the capital. They were ranged in files, forming a procession nearly two miles long. The ceremony consumed several days, and seventy thousand captives are said to have perished at the shrine of this terrible deity.

It is no wonder that Fanny Calderon de la Barca, in her *Life in Mexico,* wrote of "these bloodstained sanctuaries."

Even today one gets an emotional shock viewing the sacred cenote, or well of sacrifice, at Chichen Itza in the Yucatan, where young maidens were sacrificed to the Mayan gods. Here the Mayan priests threw the sacrifices, stupefied with hallucinatory herbs, into the murky waters of the oval-shaped natural well. Laden with jewels and precious stones, the young victims sank to their deaths, to become brides of the gods, and bring thereby an end to drought or famine or pestilence, or bring victory at war to their people.

Now, all this savage, barbarous "worship" would seem only strange and exotic, were it not for the modern cruelty that has resulted from warped religious notions. Nazi Germany of the 1930s and 1940s showed us what the devil can *still* do, using religious perversion and political atrocity.

Nazi Nightmare

Elements of the world's greatest nightmare can, disturbingly, be traced to occultic rootstock. How could a nation that gave us Luther, Beethoven, and Goethe also give us Hitler and his twisted dream of a Third Reich? How could any civilized group, however brutal, undertake to exterminate the entire Jewish race, as the Nazis did? Future generations of psychologists and social analysts will continue to search for acceptable answers to those questions. But, make no mistake about it, the elusive answer to the enigma will have, in the end, religious implications as twisted as the dream, and as convoluted as the Nazi scheme of death.

Hitler, with the strange mesmerizing power of so many tyrants, was able to lead a highly civilized people in the most monstrous enterprise of death in history. Not only did he make a quasi-religion of the Nazi state (as the Communists have also done in Russia and China), but he steeped his brain in the occult and with Germanic myths of an Aryan super-race that would dominate the world. Strangely, the grotesque war god of German antiquity, Wotan, reappeared in the Nazi nightmare to inflame a people into plundering the world. In the end, the thirty-five million souls killed in World War II lay dead under his blood-soaked feet.

In his authoritative *The Rise and Fall of the Third Reich,* William L. Shirer, a respected journalist of the era, talks about Hitler's addiction to the violent epic myth, *Nibelungenlied,* which touched a responsive nerve in the German soul:

Siegfried and Kriemhild, Brunhild and Hagen—these are the ancient heroes and heroines with whom so many Germans liked to identify themselves. With them, and with the world of the barbaric, pagan Nibelungs—an irrational, heroic, mystic world, beset by treachery, overwhelmed by violence, drowned in blood, and culminating in the *Goetterdaemmerung,* the twilight of the gods, as Valhalla, set on fire by Wotan after all his vicissitudes, goes up in flames in an orgy of self-willed annihilation which has always fascinated the German mind and answered some terrible longing in the German soul. These heroes, this primitive, demonic world were always, in Mell's words, "in the people's soul."

Actually, the rise of Nazism was abetted by a bewildering assortment of occultic and myth-worshipping cults that flourished in Germany in those awful days of civilized barbarity. These societies were dedicated to the perfection of a superintelligent race of supermen—dominant, massive, strong, and independent of Christian ties and influence.

From the dark and littered mind of Hitler, when he was still a young man (though of growing delusion), came the Nazi flag, emblazoned with the swastika. This hooked cross, which was to become the frightening symbol of Nazism, had been known since ancient times as a religious emblem. With its arms pointing clockwise, as the Nazi version did, the swastika is said to acknowledge Satan and the powers of evil.

A counterclockwise position acknowledges the power of God, *opposing* the powers of evil—very likely the ordinary pattern of the swastika. (In the early days of Nazism, it was believed by some knowledgeable observers that the Party had inadvertently adopted the wrong position for the arms of their emblem. In the light of what followed, as the Nazis lived out their *Nibelungenlied,* the conclusion is inescapable that their design was deliberate, after all.)

It can be said that the world's greatest bloodbath was essentially a pagan, anti-Christian enterprise, motivated by a warped sense of destiny, inspired by Satan's gods, and directed against the people of God. *Hitler and the Nazis—The Evil That Men Do,* Arnold P. Rubin's survey of the Holocaust (the campaign to eliminate the Jews), makes an interesting and important point that should not be overlooked:

> But the subsequent rise and fall of this archfoe of humanity has also been explained in mystical and supernatural terms. Certainly Hitler and the Nazis surrounded themselves with Germanic legends and myths. The Nazis even went so far as to set up their own occult department in government. Hitler's Viennese days served to introduce him to the occult, black magic, astrology, pornography, anti-Semitic literature, and evidently, drugs. Furthermore, Hitler decided to oppose both Judaism and Christianity, the latter growing out of the former.

Hitler was the devil's dupe, a tool in Satan's service who dreamed of being something more. This "devil in human flesh," as he was sometimes called, was barbaric and pagan to the end. As Shirer says, "It is not at all surprising that Hitler tried to emulate Wotan when in 1945 he willed the destruction of Germany so that it might go down in flames with him."

Modern Madness

Satan's delusion of unwary souls frequently involves his age-old enticement that men can be gods—an echo of his own arrant desire to be God. It has always plagued the human mind that it is possible for men to become like gods. Satan first used this ploy in his temptation of Adam and Eve in the Garden of Eden (Genesis 3:5).

It is exceedingly devilish when Satan succeeds in implanting a notion of deity, and then reverses the insanity and makes the would-be god into a monster. When this happens, the stage is set for evil beyond human understanding. The Pharaohs, who were worshipped as gods, were unfeeling brutes. The divinity-claiming Caesars were sadistic tyrants. And today's would-be messiahs are, tragically often, maddened monsters.

Perhaps the most startling and contradictory pretensions to deity have been reserved for our own time. Certainly, we live in the time when "evil men and seducers shall wax worse and worse, deceiving, and being deceived" (2 Timothy 3:13). The seductions of today are of shocking proportions—sometimes merely bizarre, sometimes vicious.

The case of the "Manson family" defies comprehension, until it is understood in its religious context. In late 1969, the world was shocked by the vicious ritualistic murders committed by this band of drug-maddened, "messiah"-led youths in California. Looking at their faces in the newspaper, you could see little difference from the decent youths of their generation. Yet, at the behest of their hypnotic leader, Charles Manson—who was recognized by his followers as Jesus Christ or God— they committed some of the foulest deeds of violence of recent times. Without sense, without pity, they went on a rampage of murder and slaughter. And yet, later, one of their number, Susan Atkins, could say, "We felt that society was destroying itself but that we were immune because we were in 'the Thought.' The early Christians had referred to themselves as being in 'the Way'; we were in 'the Thought.' We were tuned into God—at least Charlie was, and the rest of us through him."

The miasmic hold Manson had on his followers is seen in other statements from members of his "family" of murderers:

I eventually wandered out to the bus. Charlie was there, alone. He was dressed in a long white robe. I immediately knew that he might be God himself; if not, he was close to him.

In a stoned condition, I looked at Charlie across the room. The men were clustered around him. I counted; there were twelve. In his lengthening hair and beard, his eyes staring intently from face to face, he looked like Jesus talking to his twelve apostles. The thought simultaneously startled and thrilled me. I felt he might be Christ.

SUSAN ATKINS with BOB SLOSSER
Child of Satan, Child of God

The killers would later explain their insatiable lust for death, blood, and murder in a strangely demonic way: "There was a so-called motive behind all this. It was to instill fear into the pigs and to bring on judgment day, which is here now for all. . . . If you can believe in the second coming of Christ, Manson is he who has come to save" (from *Helter Skelter* by Vincent Bugliosi with Curt Gentry).

When such hideous perversions of the Christian name are made, the devil's cause is well served. A psychiatrist described the conditioning responsible for such demonic behavior as "a shared madness within a group situation." Thus Satan takes advantage of human longings and corrupts them to whatever extent he can.

The horrible Manson episode can best be understood in terms of the holy Scriptures: it was a case of demon-possession in the extreme. One of the murderers, who became a Christian while in prison, wrote later of the evil presences within her:

I was aware of other persons within me. I had often sensed that I was in other people, but at that moment I actually saw the dark, indistinct shapes within me. They were alive, moving, talking, laughing. I immediately recognized them as the same beings I had sensed in Charlie. My imitation of Charlie was perfect because we had the same things inside us.

SUSAN ATKINS
Child of Satan, Child of God

Fatal Paradise

The deceptive capacity of Satan is seen in a different setting, where a dream of paradise came to a bitter, violent halt in the closing weeks of 1978. It happened when a misguided body of lonely, displaced seekers after peace and prosperity followed a charming but deluded zealot into the jungles of Guyana to establish a socioreligious paradise. There, they dreamed and worked and planned—and dreamed some more. And there, 913 of them died. The dream ended in a death spasm of suicide and murder, in a scene of such carnage that the piled-up dead resembled the fallen in war.

The dream began with one Jim Jones, an extremely persuasive minister who elicited from his followers an uncommon dedication to himself and his theories. At the People's Temple in San Francisco, his devotees became fired with visions of paradise on earth, a utopia of peace and harmony. But gradually, the leader began to merge his ego and identity with those of Jesus Christ Himself. That madness grew, until the burgeoning messiah became a law unto himself. Jones's people, prodded by his unctuous teachings, began also to confuse the man with the Christ whom he had once served. Many followed him blindly, surrendering to him their minds and means and souls.

Jones ruled the people by means of psychological tyranny and induced fear. Clarity was soon lost, and confusion followed. In time, Jones was perceived by many to be Christ—a divine person, whose life and teaching constituted the only standard by which he or they could be judged. It was said of him that he was a god, that he was Christ reincarnated. Ultimately, he personally proclaimed himself to be Jesus Christ, or God.

Following the tragic scene of self-immolation in Guyana, Phil Kerns—a former Jones follower now a Christian—recalls in *People's Temple—People's Tomb* how some of Jones's followers regarded him:

"Maybe he is the Christ."

"All my life, I've been looking for the Christ. Not some invisible character—but a person."

"Jim Jones doesn't talk about Jesus—he is Jesus."

"Jim Jones is the only god I've ever known."

In 1977, he went to the tropical South American country of Guyana, where he established a commune for his deluded cult. He and his followers hacked a shabby Eden out of the jungle, and settled down there with their dreams of splendor. In the end, the dream was shattered, and Eden became a hell of mass suicide: Those who had once dreamed of milk and honey now drank a vile concoction of potassium cyanide and potassium chloride. Their bloated bodies were returned to a morgue in the United States; their sanctuary returned to the jungle out of which it had been hewn.

Authority and Apostasy

From the beginning of days to the present, the pattern of apostasy is the same: Satan does not stop worship—he perverts it, and turns it to error; he pollutes it, and makes it mean; he redirects it, from God to himself. He takes advantage of man's worshipful nature, twisting it to his own ends. That is the way of apostasy old and of apostasy new.

Man, made in the image of God, forever hungers for the Father. In every heart, there is a need for the security of authority, best personified in a strong father image. It is important to our understanding of this to note that such men as Charles Manson, Jim Jones, and others we shall consider later appeared to be, each in his own way, a fatherly, strong, ultimate authority.

God made us that way. From childhood to old age, we need the assurance and confidence that a father, or father-like authority, affords. The ideal resolution of that need is found in God the Father, who is at once the purpose of and the answer to our human need. The lack of an appropriate authority to attract and anchor men leads to all kinds of pernicious substitutes. And Satan is more than happy to step in and fill the void: *He* will be the father to those who will have no other.

7

Masters of Deceit

During World War II, Joseph Goebbels, the Nazi propaganda minister, theorized that when a lie is big enough, bold enough, spoken often enough, people will believe it, no matter how incredible it is. As a matter of fact, his shrewd contention was that the masses will believe a big lie more quickly than a small one. The contemptible little propagandist wrote, "Propaganda has only one object—to conquer the masses. Every means that furthers this aim is good; every means that hinders it is bad."

This callous attitude reflected Goebbels' general contempt for the human race—a contempt that showed up frequently in his voluminous diaries:

As soon as I am with a person for three days, I don't like him any longer; and if I am with him for a whole week, I hate him like the plague.

I have learned to despise the human being from the bottom of my soul. He makes me sick in my stomach.

The human being is a *canaille* [dog].

The more I get to know the human species, the more I care for my [dog].

By the clever application of his propaganda theory, the Mephistophelian Goebbels in effect brainwashed a nation—and well nigh a world. He was chief architect of one of the most monstrous and evil organizations the world has ever seen. By this deception of a nation, as I mentioned in the previous chapter, the Nazis gained power and led Germany to the brink of oblivion; by deception of the world, they carried forward their diabolical scheme to exterminate the Jewish race; by deception of themselves, they imagined their cause to be right and righteous. With them, as with all men, the ultimate deception was of themselves.

The Father of Deceit

Long before Goebbels conceived his "big lie" theory, his master—the devil—had developed deceit as his most effective device. With lies, he has achieved the destruction of millions. The primary ingredient of apostasy is deceit, the stock-in-trade of the devil, whom Jesus called an arch-deceiver, a murderer, and a liar. The intensity and pointedness of the Lord's statement to the Pharisees should be noted, especially as it appears in *The Living Bible:*

Why can't you understand what I am saying? It is because you are prevented from doing so! For you are the children of your father the devil and you love to do the evil things he does. He was a murderer from the beginning and a hater of truth—there is not an iota of truth in him. When he lies, it is perfectly normal; for he is the father of liars.

John 8:43, 44

Here, Jesus—grieved at the Jews' rejection of the truth—charged passionately that they were deceived and deluded by the devil. Their understanding had been obfuscated by the deceiver, whom they followed blindly, unable to see the truth. In modern parlance, they had been brainwashed.

In Revelation, the devil is repeatedly referred to as a deceiver: "Satan, which deceiveth the whole world" (Revelation 12:9); "the devil that deceived them . . ." (20:10); "[he] deceiveth them that dwell on the earth" (13:14); "he deceived them that had received the mark of the beast" (19:20).

The truth is that Satan's *modus operandi* has been from the beginning, is now, and shall be to the end an unrelenting use of deceit. Because of him, men die daily, never knowing what destroyed them.

The Hidden Barb

Deceit, especially that of apostasy, is like the ingenious device used by Arctic Eskimos to kill wolves, bears, and other prey. They take a long sliver of whale bone, sharpen its edges to the keenness of a knife blade and its ends to the points of daggers, and then soften it until it is pliable enough to be bent without breaking. The lethal barb is then frozen in a coiled position, embedded in a chunk of meat or blubber, and placed where the desired prey will find it.

The hungry beast gulps down the savory morsel, pleased that something so pleasant is so easily had. He does not know he has swallowed the agent of his own destruction. As the warmth of his body thaws the frozen meat, the resilient and razorsharp bone springs back to its original shape, piercing the stomach of the animal. The bleeding creature is slowly, painfully, killed by the deadly blade that he cannot disgorge, cannot see, cannot identify—cannot even know how he came to have it. For he never associates his sad state with the tasty morsel he lately relished by the side of the trail.

The deceptions of Satan are like that, as the master deceiver, the purveyor of heresy, the father of lies, hides his fatal darts in pleasant guises. He panders to the desires, inclinations, and weaknesses of his prey. Christians, aware of his evil devices (2 Corinthians 2:11), are secure from his deceptions. The world, however, is filled with persons willing to be deceived, so long as the deception is pleasant or fulfilling (at least for the present) or titillating to the spirit. So, the world is also filled with deceptions—damnable, for the most part—that appeal to every human temperament and need.

Division, Diversion, Duplication

Seizing on man's inherent need to worship (which stems from the fact that man is made in the image of God), the devil has filled the world with alternate forms of worship . . . with a confusing babble of heresy. The satanic scheme is to conquer the cause of Christ by means of division, diversion, and duplication. Much has been said about *division* in the church: for a divided body is weak and defenseless. Paul warned that "if ye bite and devour one another, take heed that ye be not consumed one of another" (Galatians 5:15). And when Christians devour one another with suspicion, criticism, jealousy, or with other emotion they do for the devil what he cannot do himself (1 Peter 5:8).

Much is said today, and with good reason, about the breakdown of morals, basic honesty, and righteous living. That is appropriate, for these must be kept in constant repair, lest Christian integrity be lost. But there are other breakdowns that equally threaten the cause of Christ: the loss of faith, fellowship, confidence, or love. When we are divided by a breakdown of inter-personal relationships, the Body of Christ is weakened and vulnerable before the devil's attacks—and nothing invites his intense opposition more than schism and division where there should be spiritual unity.

Diversion is another important tactic of the devil in his warfare against the Church of Jesus Christ. This is the focusing of attention on one matter while another of greater moment passes unnoticed. One of the most conspicuous examples of diversion is the obsessive concern with social issues while doctrinal impurity creeps into the Church, unnoticed and unchallenged. In other sectors of the Christian community, the overweening focus has been on the intrusions of worldliness, while the Church becomes increasingly immobile, due to legalism and spiritual rigidity.

The third great danger is *duplication,* probably the worst of the three. Certainly, it is the most confusing, and the surest way to victory for the devil. What he cannot deny, he imitates; by imitation, he achieves the same result as a successful denial. The adverse effect of rampant duplication can be seen in the analogy of counterfeit money: a flood of bogus twenty-dollar bills creates suspicion and distrust of the genuine article.

In religion, such suspicion quickly becomes rejection. That is why the devil is so admirably served by hypocrisy, and is so active in promoting falsehood in the Church. If Christ is the source—and the only source—of man's salvation, as He is, then the most effective opposition is not denial of Him, but duplication of His claims! That way, there will soon be so many Christs that the masses will be deceived by them. The devil is, therefore, very active in supplying false Christs, as well as false prophets, false angels, false doctrine, false miracles—total false religion. Satan's modern strategy is to "flood the market" with the false, and thereby neutralize the true. That is a dark thread running through the pattern of apostasy.

Christians may cry in confusion, "How can I avoid the trap of deception?" Let me hasten to assure you that no Christian need ever be deceived, as we shall see in a later chapter.

False Christs

Jesus warned that many would follow Him with claims of being the Messiah, with outward appeal but inward deceit:

And then if any man shall say to you, Lo, here is Christ; or, lo, he is there; believe him not: For false Christs and false prophets shall rise, and shall shew signs and wonders, to seduce, if it were possible, even the elect.

Mark 13:21, 22

Modern claimants to deity—and they have appeared regularly since the fifteenth century—have been of several

kinds. Some have claimed to be Jesus Christ reincarnated, or
returned to earth; others have claimed to be the Jewish Messiah; while still others have claimed to be Christ in conjunction with other, usually prophetic identities. During the past
century, there has been a virtual parade of these pretenders
to divinity.

In 1875, a Congregational minister's daughter, Dora
Beekman, of Rockford, Illinois, claimed to be the immortal
reincarnation of Jesus Christ. Her claim won her many converts, who hardened into a sect following her death.

In 1888, one A. J. Brown of Soddy, Tennessee, was proclaimed by his followers to be Christ. Brown himself sup-
ported the claim, and disappeared into the mountains for
forty days and nights of fasting. When he dramatically reappeared, clad in white, hands uplifted, the people rushed to
him, knelt before him, kissed his feet, and declared themselves healed of their various infirmities by his touch.

There were several other false Christs during that period,
but it is pointless to tax our minds with them.

The frequency of false Christs increased after the turn of
the century. A widely reported case in 1926 concerned the
claim of Annie Besant, leader of the sect of Theosophists,
that a Hindu named Krishnamurti was the Messiah. He was
regarded to be the embodiment of the returned Christ.

Among the numerous false Christs who appeared in many
parts of the Christian world the most striking was Father Divine, leader of an American messianic movement that was
strong from the 1930s to the 1960s. The flamboyant black
messiah had a reputed following of millions who hailed him
as God. Until his death in 1965, Father Divine reigned in his
New York "heaven" and enjoyed the luxuries heaped upon
him by his devoted followers. Next to the highly publicized
Divine—who was originally George Baker of Savannah,
Georgia—all later messiahs have been little noted by the
public, as well as markedly less sensational in their claims. A

Father Divine is a phenomenon not repeated in every generation.

Yes, the false Christs continue, and shall occur until our Lord Himself returns. Yet it is not those who overtly claim to be Christ, reincarnated or returned to earth, who pose the greatest danger to our generation. Those pretenders—and there have been several in this generation—receive only an amused attention by the news media, and in any event are followed by only a relatively few unstable or eccentric souls. The danger of these false Christs, who make interesting or entertaining newspaper copy, lies in the added confusion they bring to the religious scene. Indeed, their greatest harm may be that they divert attention from and examination of those who are false Christs *in works* (rather than in relatively harmless claims). In this way, the devil hides the hand that is doing the greatest mischief to an unknowing world.

In Christ's warnings that false Christs shall come, we are cautioned against being deceived: "For there shall arise false Christs, and false prophets, and shall shew great signs and wonders; insomuch that, if it were possible, they shall deceive the very elect" (Matthew 24:23). This is a grim, frightening prophecy—that deceit will be so effective that even the best Christians will be endangered. And, we near the end of the age, the acceleration of apostasy will reach such a dizzying and confusing pitch that virtually no one will be unaffected. Not all will be deceived, to be sure, but all will be witness to the deception, and touched in one way or another by its effects.

The Cultic Craze

The apostasy has already begun in earnest; the evidence mounts daily before our eyes. Not since the early days of Christianity, in such places as Rome, Corinth, and Ephesus, has there been a proliferation of cults, each pressing its cultic views with fervor, such as we observe about us today. Young men and women on street corners and in shopping centers, in airports and other public places, approach us with smiles and witticisms, soliciting contributions or urging their literature upon us. But take heed, for the barb of heresy is often buried in attractive fruit.

We are warned about "deceitful workers" (2 Corinthians 11:13), who claim to be—and by all outward appearances are—true ministers of Christ. Yet they are false apostles, deadly, despite any attractiveness or surface appeal they may have. Even the brightness of angels cannot nullify the devilish curse of their works (2 Corinthians 11:14, 15; Galatians 1:8). The fruit of spiritual deceit and error is poisonous, no matter how delectable it seems to be.

The cultic craze began along with the drug culture of the 50s. Ironically, in fact, some of the present cults began as apparently sincere efforts to counteract the menace of drugs, only to degenerate into something of equal, or even greater, menace. We will look briefly now at some of these cults—beginning with a movement that calls itself, chillingly, the Children of God.

Children of God   In 1968, a Christian and Missionary Alliance minister named David Berg began, with a few friends, an outreach ministry to the "hippies" of Huntington Beach, California. He recruited young Christian zealots to assist him in the rescue and rehabilitation ministry. As the ministry grew, Berg—grandly misinterpreting the Scriptures— organized colonies, or communes, in which the devotees lived. The Children of God, as they called themselves, forsook all to follow Jesus, abandoning churches, families, friends, jobs, schools, and turning over their personal possessions to the organization, to be shared in common. The organization, with its evangelistic zeal and message of love, grew marvelously, so that, today, there are eight hundred Children of God colonies in seventy countries.

As often happens, though, the good became perverted, twisted, corrupted into something unbiblical, unholy—and dangerous. Berg began to assume the identities of Moses, a latter-day prophet, and David, king of Israel. His vulgar communications to the communes—called "MO letters"— were, according to his absurd logic, the Word of God for today (as compared with the Bible, which now became the Word of God for yesterday). In addition, the having all things common began to include wives, husbands, and the connubial bed. The love the Children of God expressed so ardently soon degenerated into sex for Jesus' sake. Young female evangelists offered their bodies as love offerings to those whom they would convert. They even spoke, with unintended cynicism, of being "hookers for Jesus."

In this specious, blasphemous effort to relate to people whom they wish to convert, the Children of God use foul language, filled with obscene four-letter expletives. Perversely, those who call themselves Children of God employ profanity, free love, concubinage, and prostitution in their effort to show their love of Christ.

The ubiquity and aggressiveness of the cult increase its danger to this generation. For instance, its tentacles reached into Lee College, where I am president, in the summer of 1975. Lee is a determinedly Christian college, where the teachings of Christ are a way of life. Located in Tennessee, it is a gracious Southern campus of lawns and trees and sun and fellowship. Yet one of our lovely coeds was lured from us when representatives of the Children of God, soliciting and recruiting, descended upon the area to encourage "total commitment to Christ." Only after long, patient effort by her parents was Cyndi eventually rescued from her spiritual abduction. (Her story is told graphically by her mother, Lee Hultquist, in her book *They Followed the Piper.*)

Hare Krishna Society When members of an Oriental cult first began active evangelism in the United States it was viewed as a joke, which no one could take seriously. After all, everyone *knew* that Americans send missionaries to the Orient to convert the people from paganism—not they to us! They couldn't be serious. But a Hindu monk named Swami Prabhupada was very serious when, in 1965, he introduced his International Society for Krishna Consciousness to New York City. Working out of his store-front mission, he began his Hare Krishna teaching with public chanting in Greenwich Village in 1966, and the cult began to pique the public attention and to win converts. From there, it quickly spread across the country to the Haight-Ashbury district in San Francisco, where a second center was established. Today, with fifty temples in the United States and others in Europe, Hare Krishna has become an Eastern religious presence in a Christian culture to be regarded seriously indeed.

Wearing Oriental garb, their heads shaved, devotees of the cult peddle their literature and other articles to finance their movement. With growing boldness, behind plastic smiles, the Krishna converts badger the public in airports and other public places for donations, ostensibly to fund their numerous cultic ministries. A former member refers to their high-handed fund-raising tactics—using flattery or verbal abuse, as the particular occasion requires—as "transcendental trickery."

The central teaching of the cult is that Krishna is a personal god, present in any medium he chooses—wood, stone, marble—especially in those things made and cared for by his followers. Krishna is also incarnate in people, and has been so for five thousand years or more. Although Krishna is the official god, Swami Prabhupada, the guru of the cult, is also accorded godlike devotion and reverence by the Krishna devotees.

Transcendental Meditation Another Eastern religion growing in Western soil is TM—Transcendental Meditation—incorporated in California in 1959. Its founder, Maharishi Mehesh Yogi, received the technique of TM in a cave in India, and brought the message to America when it did not catch on there. This system of deep meditation helps the devotees to achieve "bliss consciousness of absolute being." The god of TM is the impersonal creative intelligence, which develops through a cycle of incarnations and reincarnations. By looking deeply within himself, man discovers his creative intelligence and thereby sloughs off his ignorance and indifference. It is then, too, that he establishes unity with the god of the inner person.

There are now about six thousand TM teachers, and the movement has a whopping annual income of some $20 million. As it gradually discards its religious pretenses, however, it increases its potential for danger as an implicit doctrine that God is unnecessary for spiritual awareness.

The Unification Church Still another cult that came to America from the Far East is The Unification Church, which is possibly the best known of the latter-day heresies. It was founded in Korea in 1954 by Sun Myung Moon, a millionaire industrialist, who introduced the cult to America in 1971. It had notable increases in Korea and Japan before moving its headquarters to this country in 1973.

Moon, of Presbyterian background, has wandered far from his Christian roots, although for a brief period he regarded his movement not only as Christian, but as one that would unify all the Christian churches. That lofty aim, if it was ever seriously held, had a short life. The "Moonies," as the adherents are called by the public, follow a creed that is a potpourri of biblical teaching, oriental philosophy, and personal ideas of Sun Myung Moon. New converts are won to the movement through an aggressive recruitment program, which includes mass rallies and college campus evangelism. Not averse to outright deception, the Moonies operate under an umbrella of numerous related organizations. They raise funds through a program of what some call *heav-*

enly deception, along with the sale of flowers, candles, peanuts, gensing tea, and the like. One way in which they are reputed to practice heavenly deception is by the solicitation of money for certain "worthy programs," when there are in fact no such programs, or none of any significance.

The Moonies practice communal living, in common with most of the current crop of cults, with the added flourish of mass marriages of couples that Moon has personally paired up.

Today, Moon speaks of a trinity of religions: Judaism, Christianity, and The Unification Church. He believes that there must be a worldwide religio-political movement—with him as the leader, naturally. His followers presume that he is the Messiah (a belief he does not discourage). In fact, he alludes to "mistakes" Jesus made, such as His failure to use political power or to build a material empire. Moon's Unification Church not only seems willing to use both of these secular techniques, but seems to be succeeding. Moon reportedly has a worldwide following of more than two million, with thirty thousand members and seven thousand workers in the United States alone.

But the Moonies, the Children of God, TM, and Hare Krishna are only the tip of the iceberg of false religion. There are more, many more, major and minor cults in our Christian world today. Altogether, there are about 2,500 cults at work in America alone, with a combined membership in excess of three million. They include such movements as the Jesus People, the Divine Light Mission, the Way, Church of Scientology, the No Name Group, Eckankar— the Faith of Total Awareness, and a bewildering host of others. The Caribbean Islands add still more bizarre names to the appalling list: the Rastafarians in Jamaica, Voodoo in Haiti and other lands, Mita in Puerto Rico, *ad infinitum.*

This collective confusion is Satan's handiwork; it provides a fertile field for him, while it imposes increased difficulties upon the Church. One thing is abundantly clear: *The devil is not antireligious, only anti-Christian.* He is very religious indeed, in his way, and gains glory and a certain triumph when true religion is perverted.

The devil has provided a virtual supermarket of religions for these last days. And the people, lonely and hungry, are buying.

8

Revival of the Occult

Satan must really be desperate, judging from the way he has trundled out his big guns to use against the Church. The Bible has foretold what his intensity will be like when he sees his time is short: "Woe to the inhabitors of the earth and of the sea! for the devil is come down unto you, having great wrath, because he knoweth that he hath but a short time" (Revelation 12:12). Although the fulfillment of that Scripture has not yet come, there is at present a tremendous new surge of satanic energy in the earth. This intensified evil suggests that an all-out attack has been launched against the Christian faith.

Along with the false Christs and false prophets, there is an added dimension of deceit in this generation—a renewal of occultic belief and practice in Christian lands. As I pointed out earlier, belief in the occult—supernatural powers and hidden knowledge that do not come from God—flourished during the Middle Ages, then pretty much passed into oblivion. Witches, demons, sorcery, black magic, white magic, and the like became curiosities of the past. Following man's morbid obsession with demonic powers during the period from the thirteenth to the sixteenth century, his belief in (and fear of) the occult waned, to something between whimsical curiosity and outright unbelief. Witches and demons took a back seat to the onward rush of science and technology, until the middle of our century. But now the powers of the past have come back to torment the present in full force: it is estimated that twenty million Americans and Europeans are presently involved in some form of occultism.

In its recent study of the occultic revival, *Time* magazine said:

For all its trivial manifestations in tea-leaf readings and ritual geegaws, for all the outright nuts and charlatans it attracts, occultism cannot be dismissed as mere fakery or faddishness. Clearly, it is born of a religious impulse and in many cases it becomes in effect a substitute faith.

Much of the occult, after all, is man's feeble attempt to become *god-like,* to master the world around him.

The Biblical View

Witchcraft, satanism, necromancy, and other black arts were present in Bible times, and were forbidden—first to the Jews, and then to the Christians as well. As Israel drew near to Canaan, where demon spirits were prominent in the idolatrous worship of the inhabitants, God commanded the Israelites to avoid the contamination while eliminating the evil occultic practices. The black arts are definitely the handiwork of Satan, never to be followed by the people of God. As such, they are repeatedly condemned by Scripture.

Thou shalt not suffer a witch to live.

Exodus 22:18

There shall not be found among you any one that maketh his son or his daughter to pass through the fire, or that useth divination, or an observer of times, or an enchanter, or a witch, Or a charmer, or a consulter with familiar spirits, or a wizard, or a necromancer. For all that do these things are an abomination unto the Lord. . . .

Deuteronomy 18:10–12

Regard not them that have familiar spirits, neither seek after wizards, to be defiled by them: I am the Lord your God.

Leviticus 19:31

And the soul that turneth after such as have familiar spirits, and after wizards, to go a whoring after them, I will even set my face against that soul, and will cut him off from among his people.

Leviticus 20:6

We speak of witches in a general way, but there are subtle distinctions in occultic ranks. Witches are females who practice sorcery—the use of supernatural powers of the devil—while the males are called wizards, warlocks, or simply sorcerers. Therefore, in the case of Simon, we see the words "sorcery" and "bewitched" used in conjunction with each other (Acts 8:9–11).

The famous "Witch of Endor" was a diviner, or one who practiced divination—consultation with the dead in order to foretell the future (1 Samuel 28:7–9). King Saul's case was particularly tragic because he, in an earlier flush of righteousness, had ordered all diviners and wizards expelled from the land (verse 3). When he later desired counsel from Samuel, his former mentor, now dead, he assumed a disguise and sought out a diviner, whom both he and the Lord had earlier condemned.

One of the most dramatic and pathetic episodes in the Scriptures concerns a young girl with the spirit of divination (Acts 16:16–19). The girl was a slave, whose owners used her ability to foretell the future as a means of making money. The unfortunate girl followed Paul and Silas through the city of Philippi, identifying them loudly as "servants of the most high God," until her presence moved Paul to exorcise the demon from her—as a result of which she could no longer, of course, foretell the future. (It should be observed that the words "divination" and "soothsaying" are used together, as both refer to the same occultic power—foretelling the future, or fortunetelling.)

Divination, according to the number of scriptural injunctions against it, was one of the most common occultic practices in Old Testament times (1 Samuel 6:2; Numbers 22:7; Numbers 23:23; 2 Kings 17:17; Ezekiel 13:23). One of the chief functions of diviners was to advise kings and other national rulers, who kept fortune-tellers (as we would call them) in their courts for that purpose. Among primitive peoples, these diviners were called witch doctors. Incidentally, by no means was all advice given by divination accurate. (*See* Ezekiel 13:9; 21:29; Micah 3:11.) Obviously, some diviners attained the prestige without actually having the ability!

It must be emphasized here that scriptural validation does *not* mean scriptural approval or sanction. On the contrary, all forms of occultic practice are condemned in the Scriptures. The numerous references to sorcery, witchcraft, divination, soothsaying, wizards, enchanters, and the whole occultic lot prove that such things existed, but, let it be emphasized, they were as strongly condemned as was idolatry. In fact, the two evils grew together like Siamese twins, and worked together to try to destroy and pervert the true worship of God.

Satanic Pacts

The prophet Isaiah made reference to a pact that certain self-seeking men of Judah made with Death and Hell—that is, with Satan:

You have struck a bargain with Death, you say, and sold yourselves to the devil in exchange for his protection against the Assyrians. "They can never touch us," you say, "for we are under the care of one who will deceive and fool them." . . . I will cancel your agreement of compromise with Death and the devil, so when the terrible enemy floods in, you will be trampled into the ground.

Isaiah 28:15, 18 LB

In later times, that kind of occultic agreement was called a *satanic pact,* by which a man would sell his soul to Satan in return for some temporal pleasure. Several literary plots are woven around that theme, the most widely known being Goethe's *Faust* and Oscar Wilde's *The Picture of Dorian Gray.* The Isaiah passage probably refers to the informal act on the part of certain selfish men, but in later times the satanic pact became a much more deliberate and formal procedure. In early Christian days, the beloved Augustine (who wrote ex-

tensively on demons and gods in rejoinder to the writings of
Lucius Apuleius, a worshipper of Isis) severely condemned
the practice of making pacts with the devil.

And yet the blasphemous practice grew, reaching its
height in the Dark Ages. Stories abound of pacts with
Satan— compacted in nocturnal meetings, signed in blood,
witnessed by witches—and of other infernal happenings.
The paralyzing preoccupation and superstition, of which
this was only a part, led to a gradual rejection of the whole
witchcraft scene. Occasional outbursts of hysteria, such as
occurred in France in the sixteenth century and in Massa-
chusetts in the seventeenth, were, happily, not permanent.

Satan Reappears

Now the devil has shown his hand again. In the midst of
orbiting satellites, lunar exploration, deep-space probes, jet
air travel, global television, atomic energy, and awesome
medical marvels we hear again of Satan worship, witches'
spells, spirit incantations, and a welter of attendant deviltry.
Furthermore, we can expect the demonic powers hereafter to
project themselves even more openly and boldly into our
modern society. The forces of evil will become more visible,
more blatant, and more effective than ever before—for the
devil has now brought his most sinister devices to the front.

The new interest in the occult is often an outright rebellion against spiritual authority, with spiritual connotations
that not even the practitioners discern. Converts to the occult usually come from traditional churches, and openly de-
clare their resentment with being told what to do by Christian priests or ministers. Occultic worship, they say, gives
them the freedom to do what they want, seek what they
want. They reject the Christian message of submission to
God, and seek self-assertion, self-realization, self-power. In
effect—and here is great irony—they submit themselves to
the devil while scorning submission to God.

Witchcraft   One of the precursors of modern-day witch-craft was a notorious English magician named Aleister Crowley, who died in 1947. During his lifetime, Crowley—known as "the Beast," meaning the Antichrist—did much to advance the cause of satanism. He once undertook, in apparent seriousness, to array an army of forty-nine hostile demons against Samuel Mathers, an occultic rival—and, at least among the initiates of the magical cult, it was believed without doubt that Mathers' death resulted from demonic attack!

After a lifetime of trafficking in the occult, Crowley gained a final notoriety in death, because of the pagan aspects of his cremation ceremony. The rite included a paean of praise to Pan, concluding with a blasphemous hymn of dedication to that licentious god; "Io Pan! Io Pan! Pan! Pan! Io Pan!"

In 1951, the English courts repealed that country's Witch-craft Act, an almost-forgotten law that, since 1735, had for-bidden witchcraft. Although it seemed a small matter when the law was repealed on June 22, 1951, it proved not to be so minor, in that it made witchcraft a legitimate practice in England. The reaction was immediate: Witches and wizards came out of the woodwork, and openly commenced activities that theretofore had been done in secret. They organized "Wicca"—an association of organized witch-craft—with Gerald Brousseau Gardiner as its first High Priest.

The rapid spread of modern-day witchcraft is almost be-yond belief. According to a recent survey in *Time* magazine, there are witches' covens in most parts of the United States and approximately *six thousand* covens in England, marked by a growing openness in their activities. (A coven is a more or less organized group of witches, who hold regular meet-ings and ceremonial rites.) The increase of publications de-voted to witchcraft shows the growing fascination with it. Twelve years ago, there were only five titles on witchcraft available to the public; now there are more than five *hun-*

dred—many of them "how-to" manuals on the art of witch-craft.

Satanism   Another publication of disgusting content is *The Satanic Bible,* by Anton Szandor La Vey, first High Priest of the Church of Satan in San Francisco. This grotesque orga-nization, founded in 1966, is said to number 10,000 mem-bers. Its beliefs and practices are largely an inversion of the Christian gospel—a reversal in every conceivable way of the beliefs and ethics of Christianity. An example, the priests pray to the devil, using names of biblical origin: Moloch, Apollyon, Beelzebub, Lucifer. Curses are pronounced upon the group's adversaries. Naked girls are stretched on the altars for a reverse sacrament, and human skulls are used for ornamentation.

Weird as that blasphemous hokum may be, there may be discerned a much more disturbing spread of satanism in other, more destructive ways. Groups of Satan worshippers have begun militant, physical opposition to the Church in many places. Cemeteries, church buildings, and sacred shrines have become targets for malicious vandalism and desecration in many parts of the world. The devil-worship-pers loot tombs and graves for corpses and human remains for use in their secret rites. The desecration includes such devilish symbolism as turning coffins upside down; painting black crosses on gravestones; impaling charred pigs' heads—traditional symbols of Satan—on church or cemetery crosses; and performing deviant sex rites on the altars of the vanda-lized churches. One English minister, on the occasion of his retirement in 1969, was reported by the press as saying: "In the seven years since I came to Clophill [his parish], not a month has gone by without one of the graves or tombs in the churchyard being dug up and some sort of rite performed."

A young Oregon pastor and his wife have related to me how, in 1978, they were harassed and threatened by satanists in the area. Boxes containing severed dog and cat heads and, on one occasion, a snake were left at their door. Threats of bodily harm, all in the name of Satan, became tormentingly frequent. And the threats proved real enough when the church and the living quarters where the pastor and his wife lay asleep were set afire in the middle of the night. The young couple managed to save their lives, but everything else was destroyed.

We see or read of these things in the news media and, with a gesture of disgust, pass them off as isolated acts of lunacy. Not so. They are flowing together like divergent rivulets, to become a torrent in the days ahead of us. The motivating idea of satanism is the assumption that the world is Satan's domain, ruled and controlled by him. It follows that, if he dominates the world, then Satan must in reality be God. It is therefore appropriate to worship the devil as God, and reject all Christian values as anti-Satan. By means of this heinous projection, the devil reveals that his ambition to replace God is as determined today as it was when he was Lucifer.

Future telling   In biblical terms, foretelling the future by means of some supernatural power other than God is divination. Since the future is in the hands of God, it is at best a questionable pursuit for men to try to probe its secrets. Yet, from the dim historical past, men have attempted to gain advantages by learning beforehand what will happen in the future. Practically all rulers of the ancient past relied on diviners, soothsayers, and other clairvoyants to open the future to them. In modern times, the medium most commonly used is fortune telling.

There is an intrinsic spiritual wrong in this urge, this compulsion, to know beforehand what the future holds. Once again, it is a Satan-inspired intrusion into the realm of God. The future and the past are the same to God: He sees the future as if it were already past, not something yet to be. God inhabits all of time—past, present and future—and all are one to Him. That is why He speaks of things yet to come as if they had already happened. An example is Isaiah's prophecy of Jesus' suffering, which was written in the *present* and *past* tenses seven hundred years *before* Christ (Isaiah 53:3–9). That is why we say human commerce with supernatural spirits in order to unveil the future is a clear invasion of God's omniscience.

I will not catalog all the devices men use to divine the future, which would be more wearying than productive. I should mention, however, that Christians often engage in occultic future telling without really knowing what they are doing. Indeed, some read astrology charts in all good humor, accepting the complimentary statements (forgetting that hundreds of thousands of others believe the same happy sentiments are meant for them!), and blithely dismissing all else. The danger is that consorting with the occult, even half-seriously, has a way of taking hold of a person. Many serious satanists began their blasphemies by recklessly engaging in the carnal pleasures of satanism, "for laughs," only to become ultimately convinced of the merit in what they were doing. What begins as a joke often becomes deadly serious.

Astrology—in the fortune-telling sense we are speaking of today—stems from a pagan view that the stars were gods (note that the planets of the solar system bear the names of ancient gods), and that they influenced life on earth. Thoroughly occultic in its origins, astrology has today claimed the attention of a sophisticated world. Virtually every newspaper in America carries some syndicated "horoscope" column, in which readers are treated to innocuous generalities about those born under the various signs of the zodiac.

Augustine, in his *Confessions,* acknowledged his youthful involvement in astrology, and warned Christians against the practice:

And yet, without scruple, I consulted those other impostors, whom they call "astrologers," because they used no sacrifices and invoked the aid of no spirit for their divinations. Still, true Christian piety must necessarily reject and condemn their art.

Other forms of divination, obsolete or even long forgotten, have suddenly reappeared. One, the Ouija board, which is five hundred years older than Christianity, is having a current reappearance. Sometimes a prankster's toy, at other times a serious divining device, the Ouija board is supposedly an instrument by which the dead can communicate with the living. And, although much of the imagined reaction of the mystical board is suggestive hokum, the spiritual connotations are serious.

Once again, let it be emphasized that the devil, choosing duplication from among his deceitful works, has flooded the world with every conceivable religion in order to confuse the followers of Christ. He has mixed religion and magic and heresy and lies and truth until it is sometimes difficult for honest believers to know what is right.

Keep two things forever in mind: First, behind every scheme of Satan there is a determination *to pervert true worship* and replace it with his own; that intention is behind all apostasy. Second, the deceptive traps of Satan pose no danger to those Christians who keep their place in Christ, and shun evil wherever and however it appears. Those who become trapped are those who nibble at the traps.

9

Church in the Balance

With prophetic vision, Paul foresaw that the Church will suffer severe internal defection during the last-days apostasy. That, in fact, is the essence of apostasy: a falling away from faith, a twisting of truth, an embracing of error. Pagan, cultic, and occultic influences may flourish on the fringes of iniquity, but the most harmful error is that which roots in the Church itself. That is the error that kills.

When the Church is uncertain in its sound and feeble in its leadership, the people become confused and scattered, like sheep without a shepherd. These are not the times to give indistinct or discordant sounds—to become part of the babble, to be soft and lax in spiritual leadership. The Church is needed now. And it is needed to be what it was meant to be—the body of our Lord Jesus Christ, strong and sure and certain.

The Church needs a clear and confident voice, free from fanaticism, free from negativism, free from heresy and the garble of error everywhere about us. We need to hold a steady helm in the stormy sea of apostasy. We must hold a proper course, for, make no mistake about it, the apostate waters will only grow rougher from here on out.

Unfortunately, there will be elements within the Church that will compound the forces of error. Peter, Paul, and others—even the Lord Jesus Himself—forewarned us of that fact. Jesus stated that abounding iniquity will cause the love, or spiritual dedication, of *many* to grow cold (Matthew 24:12). Paul, as I have mentioned before, warned there will be a falling away before the end-time (2 Thessalonians 2:3). But it was probably Peter who expressed it most forcibly:

There shall be false teachers among you, who privily shall bring in damnable heresies, even denying the Lord that bought them, and bring upon themselves swift destruction. And *many* shall follow their pernicious ways; by reason of whom the way of truth shall be evil spoken of.

2 Peter 2:1, 2, emphasis added

The Jews and Greeks

True faith is destined to live between two inimical forces within the walls of professing Christianity. Paul lived in just such narrows, with Jews on one side, demanding more miraculous elements in the Gospel; and Greeks on the other, demanding greater intellectual content (1 Corinthians 1:22–24). The one was emotional, the other cerebral; one elementary, the other complex. But Paul refused to see the Gospel appropriated by either extremity: He would preach the Gospel of Christ—power enough for the Jews, wisdom enough for the Greeks.

It has always been the same, up to the present day. Contradictions of our age have given voice to two opposing forces, each dangerous to the Church in its own way. The fact that each exists within the Christian pale—that each consists of faith gone awry—compounds the jeopardy of true faith. On the one side, we see a rampant, depressing fanaticism; while, on the other, we see a radical liberalism that calls itself Christian but denies the power thereof (2 Timothy 2:5).

The situation is exemplified by twin errors that spread across the land at midcentury. The two errors, being completely opposite in character, appealed to the extreme segments of the modern Christian community. On the one hand was the cynical lie that God is dead; on the other was a fanatic extravagance called the Latter Rain. The first, hyper-liberal in origin, appealed to the intellectual frustrations and cynicism of the time; while the latter, ultra-Pentecostal in character, appealed to man's intense desire to see miracles and do "greater works." Each extremity fed upon the conditions that created the other. And each in its own way tormented the body of believers, leaving a scar upon the Church which, although it is to be hoped superficial, has been slow to heal. The fire of heresy burns deep, and its embers burn long.

Between Extremes

Because the Jews and Greeks are still with us, biblical faith must exist between the tensions of the two. There are opposing ecclesiastical systems: one cold, remote and impersonal; the other fanatic, extreme, and sensate. Circumstances indicate that it will be so until the Coming of Christ, generating such dichotomous torque that the Church will be hard put to maintain its spiritual balance. Iniquity in some—who can be called Christian in only the loosest, most liberal sense—will make them agnostic (or possibly atheistic) in their faith; heretic in their doctrine; unspiritual in their hearts; formal in their worship; worldly in their living; immoral (or at least immodest) in their conduct; and self-seeking in their aims.

On the other side will be those religious extremists whose spurious claims will exceed the bounds of either Christ's demands or the necessities of spiritual order. These will be workers of deceitful miracles; promoters of quackery and sham; and those who are heretic in their doctrine, mystical in their worship, worldly in their living, immoral (or at least immodest) in their conduct, and self-seeking in their aims.

The difference between these two bodies of error is one of style more than substance, for although they are contradictory in appeal they are alike in result. All error brings similar tragic consequences to the Church, regardless of the direction from which that error comes. Because all spiritual error is destructive, it makes little difference what the reasons for it are. It is as bad to overshoot the mark as to undershoot it—both efforts miss the mark. It is as erroneous to go beyond the will of God as to fall short of it—both are outside of His will. It is as dangerous to add to the Word as to subtract from it—both distort the Gospel. In sum, there is little difference between too much and too little—both distort the body.

It is important that no heresy draw us into it so completely, or so divert our attention with fear or fascination that we fail in other Christian responsibilities. We must not allow the denials on one side to make us doubt, or extravagances on the other to make us ashamed of our identity in Christ. It is vital that the Church maintain both witness and balance between the hurtful extremes. The greater the error about us, the greater the need for spiritual sanity in our lives. For the Church to maintain its posture of truth and effectiveness it must be rooted in the Word of God; obedient to the will of God; filled with the Spirit of God; constant in prayer and supplication; consistent in faith and submission; spiritual in its living; and, finally, Godward in its aims.

No Neutral Ground

In Christ there is no neutral ground. Those who claim neutrality concerning Him are, in effect, opposed to Him. "He that is not with me is against me; and he that gathereth not with me scattereth abroad" (Matthew 12:30). Jesus set this absolute standard at the critical time when the Pharisees accused Him of casting out demons by the power of Beelzebub (Matthew 12:22–28). That blasphemy by the Pharisees was the final, fatal heresy, the ineradicable line drawn between Jesus and that iniquitous sect (verses 31–33). From that accusation onward, the schism between Christ and apostate Judaism would deepen, and the power of Christ would increase. It was no time for vacillation between opinions: Anyone unwilling to assert himself for Christ had to be reckoned against Him.

It is the same today. As the body of Christ, the Church is intended to be an extension of Him in every generation. All efforts toward neutrality lead to spiritual loss, to blurred identity and the end of effectiveness. Where the Church has neglected—or abandoned—the eternal truths that made it the Church, it has become sterile and anemic. The Church exists to proclaim the Gospel of Christ, not to live in some sterile vacuum.

Desire for neutrality by social stance on temporal matters without a corresponding spiritual leadership will inevitably lead to spiritual void. The Church exists to proclaim the truth, the faith, of Jesus Christ, to show Him as the Lord of all, and His teachings as the foundation of all truth. There can be no compromise on this responsibility, as Paul warned the Galatians:

> There be some that trouble you, and would pervert the gospel of Christ. But though we, or an angel from heaven, preach any other gospel unto you than that which we have preached, let him be accursed. As we said before, so say I now again, If any man preach any other gospel unto you than that ye have received, let him be accursed.
>
> Galatians 1:7–9

There is no middle ground for the Church. Jesus of Nazareth is the Christ, Son of the living God. Any deemphasis of that fact reduces the voice of the Church to but one more discordant sound in the babble of confusion—one more thread in the pattern of apostasy.

PART III
The Position of Believers

10

The Authority of Jesus

Satan is a master illusionist: He makes things appear to be true that are not. Illusions are deceptions—tricks of the eye and of the mind, sometimes amusing, at other times dangerous. The devil's most prevalent illusion throughout history has been the pretense that his power is equal to God's. Deceived by his sleight of hand, men sometimes imagine that there are two equal deities, one good and one evil, contending for the loyalty of man. But, make no mistake about it, that notion is a trick of the devil—there is but one omnipotence, and that is God. Satan is only a rebellious creature, who, as we shall see, will ultimately receive a rebel's punishment.

A second illusion is that the present world belongs to Satan rather than God—that God has His heaven, but Satan has the earth. That is an illusory distortion of fact. As the prince of the power of the air and the god of this world, Satan does exercise much influence, and has garnered much loyalty from men, but only to the extent that men willingly submit to his authority. He has no power over the affairs of God or over God's people; these are not subject to him in any way.

"The earth is the Lord's, and the fulness thereof . . ." (Psalms 24:1). Nothing is clearer, more precise, more emphatic than that. It is repeatedly asserted in Scripture that God owns the earth fully as much as He owns heaven. Heaven is God's throne and the earth His footstool (Acts 7:49); He is the Lord of heaven and earth (Matthew 11:25), which were made by Him (Acts 4:24). God's power is everywhere asserted upon the earth (Jeremiah 10:10–12), a fact so manifest that it needs no assertion or defense here. Any contrary thought is illusional and devilish.

Jesus on Earth

When Jesus came to earth to destroy the works of the devil (1 John 3:8), He came to a pagan world, a world of great evil and greater need, a world very much like our own. Everywhere, and in every way, He challenged the power of the devil; He set an example for us to follow, and established the premise for our victory over the forces of evil.

In a world of deceit, Jesus was truth; in a world of evil, He was righteousness; in a world of demonic power, He was the power of God. His coming to earth was a direct challenge to Satan; it signaled a time of confrontation with him and destruction of his works. In apprehension of the challenge, Satan early tempted Christ to forsake His divine purpose and thus avoid the long, hard struggle between them. That confrontation was necessary to establish the eternal supremacy of Christ over the devil, in all areas of life—on earth as well as in heaven.

The Confrontation

Although Jesus had to contend with the opposition of Satan throughout His earthly life, there was one encounter early in His ministry that was massive in effort and decisive in consequence. One gets the impression that Jesus no more relished the prospect of that confrontation than did the devil; He knew that, in the flesh, He would feel the intensity of testing as much as any man would feel it. But Jesus and Satan were compelled to meet by the express will of God, because only direct confrontation could establish the mastery of Jesus. And so they met. While Matthew 4:1 says,

"Then was Jesus led up of the Spirit into the wilderness to be tempted of the devil," I prefer the way Mark 1:12 puts it: "And immediately the Spirit *driveth* him into the wilderness" (emphasis added).

They met in the wilderness of Judea, a place so wild and forbidding that only wild beasts were there (Mark 1:13)—a place searing with heat in the daytime, and miserable with cold in the night. For forty days, Jesus was so intent upon the conflict that He had no opportunity to eat. Only when the forty days *were ended* did He hunger (Luke 4:2, emphasis added).

We are not told what occurred during those forty days, except that Jesus "was in all points tempted like as we are, yet without sin" (Hebrews 4:15). From that reference, we can only conclude that all the vile, carnal temptations that come to men came in some form to Jesus. When the forty days were ended, the devil took advantage of Jesus' physical weakness and hunger to assail His ministry with three subtle, almost imperceptible temptations. The deceiver was so presumptuous that he actually tried to lure the Lord into a corruption of His ministry; an abuse of His power; and a perversion of His allegiance to God.

The First Temptation   In the first temptation, Satan struck at a basic human need by suggesting that Jesus confirm His divinity by converting stones into bread (Matthew 4:3). This was a hidden approach, for it was certainly no sin for Jesus to partake of food, or even to produce food by a miracle. The sin would have been in the use of His miraculous powers for a selfish purpose. Although He turned water to wine for others (John 2:6–10); miraculously fed five thousand on one occasion, four thousand on another (Mark 6:38–44; 8:3–9); and caused miraculous catches of fish for His disciples (Luke 5:4–6; John 21:6–8), Jesus never used His powers for Himself. In this temptation, the devil would have had the Lord

profane His divinity by undertaking to prove He was the
Son of God, for no better reason than to satisfy His physical
hunger.

The Second Temptation   The devil then tempted Jesus to
leap from a pinnacle of the temple in Jerusalem (Matthew
4:5, 6), making an irreverent use of Scripture to assure Christ
that He would be safe. Once again, this was an attempt to
pervert the ministry of Christ. The devil would have had
Jesus resort to sensationalism as a means of demonstrating
His power over all other powers, including that of gravity. In
yielding, Jesus would have corrupted His power in the attempt to manifest it. In drawing attention to Himself by so
dramatic a miracle, Jesus would have reduced Himself to
just one more Jewish wonder-worker, like those we shall observe in the next chapter.

The Third Temptation   Satan's final assault on the divinity of Christ was so blatant, so overt, so specific in its aim
that it almost defies belief. The deceiver actually suggested
that Christ "fall down and worship me" (Matthew 4:9), of-
fering all the kingdoms of the world for His homage. The in-
ducements that Satan offered Jesus had progressed from
bread to satisfy His hunger; to sensationalism, to bring Him
attention; to, finally, kingdoms and glory, to provide Him
majesty and authority.
   But there was a particularly subtle side to this third temptation: by yielding to it, the devil implied, Jesus could have
dominion over the world without going through the agony of
Gethsemane, the humiliation of Pilate's Hall, the suffering of
Calvary. The temptation was for Him to take a shortcut to
His dominion, to bypass His dreadful—and dreaded—
death by crucifixion. The deeper implication of the temptation is terrible to consider: *It would have eliminated the only
means by which man can be saved*—the sacrificial death of Christ
for the sins of the world.

Christ was eventually to have all kingdoms and glory (which are eternally His anyway), but He had to reach them through the Cross. And it is the blood of Christ, shed on the Cross, that provides redemption and salvation for the human race. If Christ had elected to save Himself from suffering, He would have abandoned mankind to certain damnation. But, let all men be glad, the temptation was no temptation at all.

When we view that third temptation alongside Lucifer's desire to replace God, we see again that his original ambition has never been discarded—nor shall it ever be. In prophecies of the end-time, we see him still seeking worship for himself by perverting the worship of God. He, by means of one known as the False Prophet, will enforce worship of the Antichrist (Revelation 13:15).

Jesus and Demons

Following the wilderness ordeal, it is recorded that the devil departed from Jesus *for a season* (Luke 4:13), which implies that there were further confrontations between them. Although there is no record of further face-to-face confrontations, there were numerous oblique encounters of other sorts. For example, Jesus came upon many demoniacs, and cast the demons out of them. The Gospels are replete with accounts of His liberation or healing of the demon-possessed, some of which are noteworthy because they provide extensive proof of spiritual authority (Matthew 4:24; 8:16, 28; Mark 1:32, 34, 39; Luke 6:18; 11:20; 13:32).

In the region of Gadara (Luke 8:26–35) for example, Jesus and His disciples encountered a man "which had devils long time, and ware no clothes, neither abode in any house, but in the tombs." His demon-possession was severe, *because many devils were entered into him*—so severe that he was known by the name *Legion*. In Roman military organization, a *legion* was a force of six thousand soldiers. As the term was used to refer to the demoniac, therefore, it meant that he was possessed by multiple demons. When Jesus cast the demons out of the man, they dispersed into a herd of swine, which—maddened by the invading demons—ran into the sea and were drowned.

Jesus' authority over the spirit world was further demonstrated in other dramatic encounters, as when He, Peter, James, and John met a demoniac on their way down the Mount of Transfiguration (Mark 9:14–19). Just as Legion was possessed with multiple demons, this youth had numerous maladies as a result of his demon-possession. In Matthew 17:15, the father called him a *lunatic.* (In the Revised Standard Version, an *epileptic.*) In Mark 9:17, the demon is called a *dumb spirit,* and in Mark 9:25, Jesus addressed it as a *dumb and deaf spirit.* During his seizures, the youth would fall, foam at the mouth, and grind his teeth. The father, in understandable distress, brough his son to Jesus' disciples, who failed to exorcise the demon. However, Jesus arrived and cast the demon out. In the course of the encounter, the youth had a violent seizure, which, combined with the exorcism, left him so still that the onlookers at first thought he was dead (Mark 9:26, 27). When he rose up, cured, and delivered from the demon, the people were "amazed at the mighty power of God" (Luke 9:43).

Neither the number nor the nature of the demons mattered to Jesus; He was master of every enemy power. A commanding figure when He addressed a demon, Jesus used expressions consistent in authority: "He *commanded* the unclean spirit"; "Jesus *rebuked* the devil"; "He *cast out* many devils"; "He *suffered not* the devils to speak." The unquestioned authority of Jesus evoked both obedience from the demons and amazement on the part of the witnesses.

Frequently, the demons indicated their recognition of Jesus with such words as, "I know thee who thou art, the

Holy One of God" (Mark 1:24); and "Thou art the Son of God" (Mark 3:11). Jesus ordered the demons to be silent, however, for He would not accept such announcement of His deity from them: Demonic voices were not fit to introduce the Son of God.

Demons and Sickness

Jesus responded to human need everywhere. Because His compassion accepted people as readily as His power attracted them, He healed many persons and delivered them from demonic bondage (Mark 1:34).

It is important to observe that, contrary to a common fallacy, all sickness was not (and, of course, is not) caused by demonic powers. Many times, Jesus indeed healed the afflicted by casting out demons (Matthew 15:22, 28; Luke 6:18; 8:2), but more often there is no mention of demon-possession among those He healed (Matthew 8:3, 6–15; Mark 5:28, 29; Luke 18:41–43). A clear distinction is frequently made between those who were possessed by demons and those sick from natural causes (Matthew 4:23, 24; 8:16; Mark 1:32; Luke 7:21).

Jesus healed diseases *and* cast out devils. They were not—and are not—the same thing. We read in the Word of God about many followers of Christ who were sick, with no suggestion of evil or demon powers: Lazarus, the friend of Jesus (John 11:3, 4); Peter's mother-in-law (Matthew 8:14); Paul's co-workers, Epaphroditus (Philippians 2:25–27); Trophimus (2 Timothy 4:20); and Timothy himself (1 Timothy 5:23); among many others.

No child of God can be demon-possessed, for one whom Christ possesses cannot be possessed by another. The fact that Satan can, under certain circumstances, afflict men does not mean that all illness is due to his interference. Sickness is a part of the natural course of life, to which all living creatures are subject: Christians and sinners alike sicken and die.

Paul emphasized that, whether in life or death, Christians belong to Jesus Christ. "Living or dying we follow the Lord. Either way we are his. Christ died and rose again for this very purpose, so that he can be our Lord both while we live and when we die" (Romans 14:8, 9 LB).

Authority Over Death

In the mortal reasoning of man, death is the greatest and most dreaded power on earth. It is the final authority that all men must acknowledge—the inexorable conqueror of all living things. Death, according to the reasoning of man, is the final truth before which we all must bow.

Admittedly, death is the consequence of sin, the fruit of rebellion that reaches back to the perversions of Satan in the Garden of Eden. Death, indeed, will be the last enemy to be destroyed, but it will ultimately be abolished from the earth (1 Corinthians 15:26; Revelation 20:14).

In the face of these facts, Jesus manifested His power over death by restoring the dead to life. He raised at least three persons from the shade of death: the widow's son in Nain (Luke 7:11–15); the daughter of Jairus (Mark 5:38–42); and Lazarus in Bethany (John 11:14–44). In these instances, Jesus invaded the precincts of death to manifest His dominion over all earthly dominions.

His greatest victory over death was when He arose from His own death and entombment, a victory of such significance and finality that all authority over the devil rests upon it. More will be said about that triumph in a later chapter.

Authority Over Sin

Christ's authority over the devil was complete, touching upon every conceivable realm of human need and satanic influence. The greatest of these exercises of authority was in the matter of sin. Christ's forgiveness of sin was the rescue of souls from the bondage of the devil—an action so bold that even the religious men of the time were astonished by it. Their questioning of His authority did not deter Him, however: He forgave all sinners who repented (Luke 7:47–50), and asserted the same authority even as He died (Luke 23:42, 43).

Just as Jesus invaded the stronghold of Satan to deliver Legion from demons, so He demonstrated His authority over sin when He forgave the woman taken in adultery (John 8:3–11). On a morning at the great temple in Jerusalem, the hypocritical religious leaders laid a trap for Jesus by bringing to Him (supposedly for His advice and judgment) a woman who had been discovered in the act of adultery. This was a frontal challenge of His authority, fortified by a recitation of the Mosaic penalty for adultery—death by stoning.

Jesus resolved the evil confrontation by writing on the ground a message that exposed the sins of the woman's accusers. It is conjectured that His words reiterated the very Law by which the woman was to be executed, revealing the guilt of those who are always ready to condemn another.

The authority of Jesus was so forcibly demonstrated on this occasion that, one by one, the guilt-smitten accusers abandoned the scene to Jesus and the woman. His forgiveness of her sins is embodied in His words, "Neither do I condemn thee: go, and sin no more."

An equally bold exercise of His power to forgive sin was His forgiveness of the palsied youth in Capernaum (Mark 2:3–11). On that occasion, His authority was not challenged overtly by antagonists (as it was in the case of the adulterous woman), but it was privately questioned by critical observers. Perceiving the nature of his detractors' criticism, Jesus validated His authority to forgive sin by two attendant manifestations of His power: He revealed the thoughts of His critics, and healed the youth of his palsy. This amounted to a show of His credentials—as Healer, Savior, and Lord.

Authority Over Iniquity

The greatest hindrance to Jesus was none of the things I have mentioned so far: those He handled with dispatch. His greatest opposition came from the religious people of His day—specifically, the scribes, Pharisees, and Sadducees. As is always the case, the most effective work of evil proceeded from religion. In Jesus' day, the Pharisees were the worst of the lot—not because they were more evil, but because they were supposed to be better. Once, the Pharisees had been an honorable body of men, called *Perushim*, the *separated ones* (or, as they preferred to call themselves, *Hasidim*, the *pious ones*). But they who had once been so worthy, they who had for so long anticipated the Messiah, they who had kept Judaism fit for His coming, were not fit themselves when He at last came. They had followed the pattern of apostasy by mingling error with truth, by substituting self-righteousness for true righteousness, by crushing the spirit of the Law with the letter of the Law.

The devil had so completely infiltrated the proud sect of the Pharisees that even harlots, drunkards, publicans, and thieves were more sympathetic to Christ than they (Matthew 21:31; Luke 18:9–14). Jesus was vigorous in His opposition to these pretentious religious leaders, whom He criticized with boldness (Matthew 5:20; 23:13–29; Luke 12:1; Mark 7:5–7).

The proud sect committed the ultimate blasphemy when they accused Jesus of casting out demons by the power of the devil: "But some of them said, He casteth out devils through Beelzebub the chief of the devils" (Luke 11:15). This profanation of God's power represented an important watershed in the ministry of Christ, who responded bitterly to the blasphemy, thenceforward identifying the Pharisees as the greatest enemies of truth and holiness. They who should have recognized that Christ's authority came from the Father committed the grievous, the unforgivable blasphemy of accrediting the authority of God to the devil (Matthew 9:34).

Jesus asserted the truth without hesitation, for the very reasons that error must be answered with truth and the power of wrong must be overcome with the power of right. Without fail, He overcame the works of the devil—sin and sorrow and sickness and death—and, in so doing, both staked a position for His people and showed us the way to attain it.

11

The Authority Extended

Jesus' authority over evil did not end with His earthly life. In fact, one of His most important works was the transmission of His ministry into the capable hands of worthy men. He gave the twelve apostles "authority over all devils" (Luke 9:1); that is, "power against unclean spirits, to cast them out, and to heal all manner of sickness and all manner of disease" (Matthew 10:1). Later, when Jesus sent seventy other disciples to preach, they returned, excited that "even the devils are subject unto us through thy name," whereupon Jesus emphasized their authority: "I give unto you power to tread on serpents and scorpions, and over all the power of the enemy . . . " (Luke 10:19).

Of all the ways Jesus asserted the apostles' spiritual power over Satan and his works, one of the most impressive was His comparison of their relationship with Him to that of a vine and its branches (John 15:1–8). Now, branches are the fruit-bearing extensions of the vine, with all of its nature, essence, and power: It is biologically impossible for the branches to be different from the vine, in either species or purpose. They are one: What the vine is, the branches must be also. Moreover, they are dependent upon each other, and only in this relationship is there any difference: The branches have life through the vine, while the vine bears its fruit through the branches. In this analogy, Jesus revealed the continuing interdependence He would have with His disciples: they would be dependent upon Him for their life; He upon them to bear His fruit. In spirit and purpose, though, they were the same.

Following His Resurrection, He promised the disciples an

110

induement of power by the Spirit (Luke 24:49: Acts 1:8), which promise was fulfilled by the Holy Spirit on the day of Pentecost (Acts 2:1-4). Beginning on that day, His disciples became His Church, an extension of His ministry, doing on earth what He would have Himself done had His earthly life continued.

Greater Works

On the evening before His crucifixion, preparatory to His leaving them, Jesus made His disciples a remarkable promise: "Verily, verily, I say unto you, He that believeth on me, the works that I do shall he do also; and greater works than these shall he do; because I go unto my Father" (John 14:12). That promise has given rise to much misunderstanding among Christians, especially in this century. Some have imagined it possible, even expected, for Christians to exceed the supernatural works of Christ—and that bit of folly has become one of the most damaging errors of our time.

That error is unfortunate for the promise is really quite simple. The word *greater* can refer to either *kind* or *extent*—as one thing can be of greater *quality* than another, or greater in *size* than another. Since it is impossible to do a greater *kind* of work than Jesus did—such as the forgiveness of sin, raising the dead, and defying the elements—it is obvious that He meant that the apostles would do work of a greater extent, of a greater *scope*, than He did. His life was cut short after a ministry of only three years—*"because I go unto my Father"*—but His followers, generation after generation, would work without end.

His ministry never reached beyond the eastern Mediterranean region of Palestine—about 140 miles at its greatest extent. But his immediate followers, the disciples, penetrated regions far removed from Palestine, all the way to Asia, Greece, and Rome. They did—and the Church continues to do today—a greater extent of work than He had time to do.

But there can be no greater *kind* of work than He did.

Early in their ministry, the apostles encountered many of the situations Jesus met, plus many He never met. First of all, just as He had done, they encountered opposition by apostate Judaism, as represented by the Pharisees. As they pressed onward, they had to face iniquitous Jewish opponents in Judea and beyond, wherever the Jews were scattered. They later encountered the determined opposition of idolatrous practitioners and occultic believers, for they went into a hostile world, without friends and without sympathy.

The early Christians did not go into the world timidly and haltingly: They went with courage and confidence. It does not befit the body of Christ to live in fear of the devil, intimidated by his agents or his works. The followers of Christ had spiritual authority to withstand all evil, and to triumph over it. They needed it. In Israel, Jesus contended primarily with organized Judaism—scribes, Pharisees, Sadducees; the apostles met that hindrance, plus Jewish opposition beyond Judea, plus the paganism of the Gentile world.

World of Iniquity

Conflict with spiritual fraudulence came early, as the Gospel of Christ attracted attention, first in Judea and then in Samaria. The power of the Gospel evoked envy and emulation among many whose false claims were threatened by it. There were several occasions where the devil tried to hinder God's work, using the imitation and deceit of Jewish charlatans.

Simon the Sorcerer   Peter's meeting with Simon the sorcerer is a case in point. Simon, a Jewish sorcerer of considerable repute in Samaria, witnessed the miracles that accompanied Philip's ministry—particularly the casting out of demons and the healing of the afflicted—and attached himself to the evangelist (Acts 8:5–13). Simon, who has long been called Magus (because that is the fifth, and highest, rank among sorcerers), was a mighty spiritual influence in Samaria. It is twice mentioned that he had bewitched the Samarians, meaning that he was a person of influence in the city. The people, deceived by his admixture of Jewishness and occultic trickery, believed Simon to be "the great power of God." The entrance of Philip into Samaria especially interested Simon, who studied the Christian message and miracles with care.

Simon, attracted by the power of the Gospel more than by its message, submitted to baptism. That he was not a true believer is evident from Peter's words to him, after the apostle had joined Philip in Samaria. Peter, accompanied by John, was not awed by the prominence of Simon; nor did he mince words when the charlatan attempted to buy the Holy Spirit (Acts 8:14–19). On the contrary, Peter spoke sharply to Simon:

> Thy money perish with thee, because thou hast thought that the gift of God may be purchased with money. Thou hast neither part nor lot in this matter: for thy heart is not right in the sight of God. Repent therefore of this thy wickedness, and pray God, if perhaps the thought of thine heart may be forgiven thee. For I perceive that thou art in the gall of bitterness, and in the bond of iniquity
> Acts 8:20–23

With spiritual boldness, Peter dared confront the sorcerer and repudiate his iniquity. Simon, a Jew who represented himself as a person of piety, was guilty of iniquity, rather than mere transgression. And because his spiritual sin was a perversion of truth, it deserved the severest condemnation.

Elymas Bar-jesus A similar incident occurred to Paul on the island of Cyprus, where a sorcerer named Bar-jesus, or Elymas, wielded an unusual spiritual influence over the Roman ruler, Sergius Paulus (Acts 13:6–8). Elymas, called "a false prophet, a sorcerer, a Jew," had gained the confidence of Sergius Paulus as a prophet of God. When the Roman dignitary heard of Barnabas and Paul (who was still known as Saul), he sent for them, and they taught him the Word of God. Sergius Paulus was called "a prudent man," which indicates that he was sincerely seeking spiritual truth. Elymas, foreseeing how his influence with the ruler would be lost, withstood the apostles and argued against them. He who was, like Simon Magus, an apostate Jew but who pretended to be a man of God, actively sought to prevent Sergius Paulus from accepting the faith of Jesus Christ.

Paul was no more intimidated by Elymas than Peter had been by Simon. Quite the opposite, for the Christian apostle flared up against the Jewish charlatan with spiritual boldness:

> Then Paul, filled with the Holy Spirit, glared angrily at the sorcerer and said, "You son of the devil, full of every sort of trickery and villainy, enemy of all that is good, will you never end your opposition to the Lord? And now God has laid his hand of punishment upon you, and you will be stricken awhile with blindness."
>
> Acts 13:9-11 LB

Paul set forth one of the clearest descriptions of iniquity to be found in the Scriptures: Elymas, who should have declared the truth, had twisted and perverted it; he who should have done the works of God, had obstructed others from doing them. Paul's condemnation of Elymas was as severe as had been Peter's of Simon, and God's judgment was even more immediate—the sorcerer was struck with temporary blindness. When Sergius Paulus saw what had happened, he was convinced of the truth and accepted the doctrine of the Lord.

Sons of Sceva   Of the many instances of religious fraud encountered by Paul, none was more dramatic and ironic than that of the sons of Sceva. Sceva, the father, was a Jewish priest in Ephesus. His seven sons were exorcists, professional casters out of devils, who obviously took advantage of their Jewish heritage to build for themselves a reputation of spiritual prowess. From what followed, it is evident that their claim of exorcistical power was pure hokum. (It is important to note that the iniquity of Simon, Elymas, and the sons of Sceva had one common element: All were Jews who took advantage of the Jewish reputation for prophetic religious power and mixed it with a gaudy pretentiousness to gain influence as servants of God.)

Paul preached in Ephesus, with tremendous spiritual results: "God wrought special miracles by the hands of Paul: So that from his body were brought unto the sick handkerchiefs or aprons, and the diseases departed from them, and the evil spirits went out of them" (Acts 19:11, 12). The vagabond Jews, astonished at such results, added the name of Jesus to their repertory of enchantments and charms. When they undertook to cast a demon out of a man who really was demonized, they failed. Beaten by the man whom they would liberate, they fled for their lives (verses 13–16).

The unintended result was that the name of the Lord Jesus was magnified in Ephesus, and both Jews and Greeks were converted to the faith. The city of Ephesus was a center for every sort of false religion—particularly the occult, and the worship of the goddess Diana. Because the sons of Sceva bordered on the occult with their mumbo-jumbo religion, what happened to them had a widespread effect among the practitioners of magical rites. These persons burned their books and deserted their magical practices, as "mightily grew the word of God and prevailed" (Acts 19:20).

World of Idolatry

As soon as the Church spread beyond the warm womb of Palestine, it met a pagan world. F. W. Worsley, in the *Dictionary of the Apostolic Church*, sums up the situation well:

So deep-rooted was the Jewish hatred of idolatry, and so general had been the condemnation of the practice, that our Lord found no reason for insistence upon the generally accepted commandments on the subject. But as soon as the gospel message began to be preached outside the pale of Judaism, the matter became one of the pressing questions of the day. . . . It is not surprising to read (Acts 17:16) that, when St. Paul visited Athens, "his spirit was provoked within him, as he beheld the city full of idols," even though the statement is not strictly accurate. His whole training rendered him antagonistic to anything approaching idolatry; and in his letters the same feeling is expressed. No Christian was to keep company with idolators (1 Corinthians 5:10), who could not inherit the Kingdom of God (1 Corinthians 6:9, Ephesians 5:5). He reminds the Thessalonians that they had abandoned the old idolatrous worship "to serve the living God" (1 Thessalonians 1:9). Yet from the Christian point of view there is only one God, and the true Christian cannot but recognize that thus "no idol is anything in the world" (1 Corinthians 8:4).

Ephesus was a prominent center of idolatry, with Diana of the Ephesians its patron deity. Diana, the goddess of Ephesus, called Artemis by the Greeks, represented the reproductive power of the human race. The pagan mind was powerfully impressed by the reproductive process, to them the greatest of all human faculties, and worshipped it— sometimes the male form, sometimes the female. The temple of Diana was a vast institution, with countless priests, priestesses, and temple-servants. The temple itself was so magnificent that it was one of the renowned Seven Wonders of the World. The cult of Artemis, wild and orgiastic in character, was by no means confined to Ephesus, however: The statement in Acts 19:27, "whom all Asia and the world worshippeth," was no exaggeration.

The Ephesians were doubly proud of the goddess: first, because she was theirs; and second, because worship of her brought to Ephesus countless visitors from all parts of the Roman Empire. This, of course, was good for trade, so that religion and self-interest went conveniently hand in hand. (The account in Acts 19:23–40 shows what extremes of enthusiasm can be aroused when religious fervor and commercial greed are united.)

Paul's preaching, with its reasoned logic and spiritual truth, drew many away from the licentious cult of Artemis. The resulting uproar against Paul was so violent that his life was in serious jeopardy. Idolatry in the days of the early Church was a serious business: When the Christian message was carried into pagan lands, it frequently generated upheavals that endangered the lives of the evangelists.

Pagan opposition to the Christian faith, determined and universal, is spoken of often in the Book of Acts and in the epistles (Acts 14:1-6; 17:16-34, 1 Corinthians 8:1-10; 1 Thessalonians 1:9). For all its prevalence, however, it is lightly treated in comparison with perversions of the true faith. While Satan motivates idolatry fully as much as heresy, the distinctions between Christ and idols are so pronounced that less warning is necessary in the first instance. Spiritual error that exists by imitation and deception is more difficult to discern, and therefore more dangerous to the cause of Christ.

The Name of Jesus

Jesus' name became—and remains—the source of Christian effectiveness and triumph over adversity. He sent His disciples into the world in His name, and instructed them to pray, speak, and work in His name. The expression *in His name* means *by His authority*. What the apostles did in the name of Jesus, they did by His authority and in His power. The Jewish rulers demanded of Peter and John, following the healing of the lame man: "By what power, or by what name, have ye done this?" (Acts 4:7). In other words, "By whose authority have you healed this man?" The forthright answer of Peter was, "by the name of Jesus Christ of Nazareth" (verse 10). Everything the apostles did was on His authority. Some nonbelievers, observing the apostles' frequent use of Jesus' name, believed it to be some magical incantation, and appropriated it to their use. The sons of Sceva made that error, to their injury and regret.

As in the past, a fraudulent use of Christ's name will occur in the last days. Workers of iniquity will pretend to have worked for the Lord, but He will expel them from His presence: "Depart from me, ye that work iniquity" (Matthew 7:23). Paul gives a further warning on the subject: "Let every one that nameth the name of Christ depart from iniquity" (2 Timothy 2:19).

There is great power, indeed, in the name of Jesus—that name which shall always be the Christian's greatest source of strength and surest recourse in time of need. More than a hundred times the New Testament assures us of the efficacy of His name, which is above every name (Ephesians 1:21; Philippians 2:9). His name has power over all the power of sin and Satan. It is the name of Jesus, and His name alone, that effects salvation for man. "And it shall come to pass, that whosoever shall call on the name of the Lord shall be saved" (Acts 2:21); "Neither is there salvation in any other: for there is none other name under heaven given among men, whereby we must be saved" (Acts 4:12).

The name of Jesus was the authority by which His disciples did many things during the course of their ministry.

They gathered together in His name (Matthew 18:20).

They cast out devils in His name (Mark 9:38; Luke 10:17; Acts 16:18).

They prayed in His name (Matthew 6:9).

They healed the afflicted in His name (Acts 3:6, 16).

They preached in His name (Acts 4:17–20; 5:28; 8:12; 9:27).

They did signs and wonders in His name (Acts 4:30).

They were tried for His name (Acts 4:7–10).

They suffered shame for His name (Acts 5:40, 41).

They risked their lives for His name (Acts 15:26; 21:13).

They baptized in His name (Acts 8:16; 10:48; 19:5).

They conducted business affairs of the Church in His name (2 Thessalonians 3:6).

Modern believers are likewise told to appropriate the name of Jesus in their daily lives: For all that the apostles did in His name, we are empowered to do today.

> Giving thanks always for all things unto God and the Father *in the name* of our Lord Jesus Christ.
>
> Ephesians 5:20, emphasis added

> And whatsoever ye do in word or deed, do all *in the name* of the Lord Jesus, giving thanks to God and the Father by him.
>
> Colossians 3:17, emphasis added

> And whatsoever ye shall ask *in my name,* that will I do, that the Father may be glorified in the Son. If ye shall ask any thing *in my name,* I will do it.
>
> John 14:13, 14, emphasis added

To pray in Jesus' name is to pray in harmony with His character; it is to keep our lives consistent with His character. Contrariwise, nothing can be truly in His name that is inimical to His nature and will. As Paul said in another age of confusion, "In him we live, and move, and have our being . . ." (Acts 17:28).

12

Upon This Rock

One of the most frequently quoted and strongly reassuring promises of Christ is, "Upon this rock I will build my church; and the gates of hell shall not prevail against it" (Matthew 16:18). In every period of distress, the Church looks to that promise of its permanence, and beyond the promise to Peter's statement that evoked it: "Thou art the Christ, the Son of the living God" (Matthew 16:16). The divinity and Lordship of Christ form the unshakable foundation of His Church. So long as all its thought and action stem from the fact of His Lordship, the Church is invulnerable to all that the devil can do against it.

The assertion, "the gates of hell shall not prevail against it," is one of the grandest statements in Scripture, and one that does not admit doubt. The figurative word *gates* harks back to ancient times, when the elders of a city held court inside the gates of the city walls. The tribunal of elders convened in that place because it was convenient to all the citizens, and there passed judgment on public, civil, and religious issues. (*See* Genesis 19:1; Deuteronomy 22:15; Ruth 4:11; Job 29:7).

Christ's promise asserts the Church's indomitable character. No device of Satan can overcome it, and all efforts of hell against the people of God are doomed to failure. Similarly, all judgments of evil against the Church must come to naught. Under the Lordship of Jesus Christ, the Christian body will prove triumphant against every appearance of evil.

The Line of Tension

All periods of history are not equal. While it is true that most things that happen today have happened in some form in the past, it is also true that life is more like an undulating line than a level plane. The pattern of history, sacred no less than profane, is a roller coaster of ups and downs, highs and lows, in the human experience. In the spiritual realm, this translates into periods of apostasy and periods of awakening; periods of advancement and periods of retrenchment.

It is an observable, traceable fact that times of special revival have, historically, been countered with intensified evil. That phenomenon is nothing less than the effort of Satan to overcome, or at least to counteract, the works of God. Naturally, the reverse is also true: Renewal of faith follows apostasy, as good men are revolted by excessive evil.

The late Jewish Christian scholar, Alfred Edersheim, in his extensive *Life and Times of Jesus the Messiah,* traced the pattern in Biblical history:

There are critical epochs in the history of the kingdom of God, when the power of evil, standing out in sharpest contrast, challenges that overwhelming manifestation of the Divine, as such, to bear down and crush that which opposes it. Periods of that kind are characterized by miraculous interposition of power, unique even in Bible-history. Such a period was, under the Old Testament, that of Elijah and Elisha, with its altogether exceptional series of miracles; and, under the New Testament [the period that followed charges] of the Pharisees against the Christ.

It is evident that ours is a day of renewed spiritual awareness, with Christian revival occurring in unexpected places. It has again become acceptable to speak in mundane society of being born again. The airwaves of radio and television—long the domain of commercial hype and God-ignoring fantasy—are now mediums for declaring the message of Christ. It is a time of growing awareness of the miraculous powers of Christ—His power to deliver from evil, heal affliction, replenish barren lives; to fill with His Spirit, straighten what was crooked, and secure from the devil's terror.

To counteract this manifestation of the Divine, the devil has intensified his efforts to seduce men and interfere with the plan of God. But we should not be alarmed by this upsurge of evil: It only confirms the validity of spiritual renewal. From the beginning of the Church, each genuine revival period has seen a frenzy of satanic opposition. In his monumental *History of the Christian Church*, Philip Schaff observed that:

> As Christ, in the days of his flesh, was hated, mocked, and crucified, his church likewise is assailed and persecuted by the powers of darkness. The history of Christianity includes therefore a history of Antichrist ... The church militant must, from its very nature, be at perpetual warfare with the world, the flesh, and the devil, both without and within. For as Judas sat among the apostles, so "the man of sin" sits in the temple of God; and as even a Peter denied the Lord, though he afterwards wept bitterly and regained his holy office, so do many disciples in all ages deny him in word and in deed.

Three such periods of revival—the Apostolic, Reformation, and Wesleyan—because of similarities to our own deserve our attention.

The Apostolic Period

The sturdy band of apostles faced a world of satanic influence beyond our comprehension. It was a time of beginning, not of mere reform, for reform is not possible where fundamental principles are at variance. As Schaff observed, "It is difficult to convert a nation; it is more difficult to train it to the high standard of the gospel; it is most difficult to revive and reform a dead or apostate church." Judaism was dead, having died even before Christ lived, and a new force was taking its place. Satan worked mightily to kill the Church aborning, to stop its penetration of the world before it was

well begun. The numerous mortal enemies of the young
Church were determined and fierce, too, so fierce that Jesus'
warning, "I send you forth as sheep in the midst of wolves,"
was more than just rhetoric. It was the truth.

Now, a wolf is a marvelous creature of destruction. Savage
and strong, a single wolf is able to kill many sheep. In ranch
country, one wolf has been known to kill more than a hundred sheep in a night. But even that fact is not adequate to
frame Satan's opposition to the Church. In literal situations,
the sheep are almost always numerous and the wolves few.
But it is the other way around in Jesus' words, where wolves
are the plurality and sheep the minority. The apostles would
be like lone sheep in a pack of wolves, in other words—not
numerous sheep with a single wolf among them.

The apostles were undaunted by such odds, however, and
went forth with confidence to conquer the world. The boldness of the Church was remarkable as it uprooted the old religions, apostate and pagan alike, and reasserted the pristine
worship of God. Satan countered with religions of every sort
and for every taste. The temples of Bacchus and Dionysus
were scenes of drunkenness and rioting, while the temple
prostitutes of Venus, Artemis, Isis, and Aphrodite proffered
their carnal services to the lustful populaces of Athens,
Corinth, Ephesus, Rome and lesser cities. The mystery faiths
of Horus, Osiris, and Mithras attracted the contemplative,
and sometimes morbid, mystics. Zeus, Jupiter, and their
companion deities held the allegiance of the aristocracy,
while Athena, Apollo, and Minerva held a lofty appeal to
the scholar and the poet.

Yet the Christian messengers refused to be discouraged or
intimidated by the magnitude of the opposition they faced.
Paul, at the behest of the Stoics and Epicureans, stood alone
and unafraid on Mars Hill, under the towering Acropolis
with its gleaming temples, and proclaimed the Gospel of
Christ. And the worship of pagan gods did not long survive
the introduction of the Christian Gospel into the ancient

world. The purer faith prevailed, as it must, while the old paganism sank into insignificance and demise, as *it* must.

The devil threw his best against the early Church—apostate Judaism, elaborate paganism, militant occultism, and brutal imperialism—and yet the Church won! It won because the daring band of Christians had love for mankind, courage, confidence in itself, and faith in its cause. Above all else, the Christians had the authority of Him who had sent them forth. And with these powerful arms, they triumphed over all opposition.

The Reformation

As the Apostolic Church triumphed in the days of paganism and apostate Judaism, so the Reformation Church of the sixteenth and seventeenth centuries triumphed over satanism and black magic. Concurrent with serious efforts to reform a Church grown materially rich and spiritually bankrupt was a demoralizing obsession with the devil and his powers. Western civilization was just emerging from the Dark Ages into the dawn of Renaissance. The Reformation, twin brother of the Renaissance, would take away the spiritual blindfolds that plagued the Church, and set it free again.

In addition to the blindfold that hindered simple Christian faith, there was a maze of superstition regarding most spiritual matters. Fear of demons and monsters burned like a fever in town, hamlet, and countryside. The period of the Reformation was a tortured time, as the devil sought to hold through fear and confusion what he was losing through faith in the Word. It was a time of witch-hunts and of the wildest fanaticism, a classic instance of Satan shoving forward what he cannot retard. For he does not care if we fall on our backs or on our faces, just so long as we fall.

So, the tangled Gordian knot of satanism, superstition,

fear, and persecution threatened to bind the lives of those seeking deliverance from a Romanism perilously akin to that Rome of the apostles' time. Luther, Knox, Zwingli, Tyndale and the determined body of Reformers, however, used the sword of the Word to cut through the tangled mass and set man's spirit free.

As might be expected, the mightiest of the Reformers, Martin Luther, seems to have been a special target of the devil. Through periods of depression and frustration, he fought inner battles no less furious than those he fought outwardly. Luther's biographers make much of his conflicts with Satan, including a widely circulated story that once, while translating the New Testament in Wartburg Castle, he became so aware of the devil's presence that he threw an inkwell at the apparition. In his excellent biography *Luther*, Rudolf Thiel says that the devil attacked Luther with his utmost power and craftiness, and thought to bring him down. Much earlier, Thomas Carlyle recorded that Luther on one occasion wrote, "I have seen and defied innumerable devils."

Edwin P. Booth, in *Martin Luther: Oak of Saxony,* says with understanding:

Devils, witches, and all the world of superstition, were his native environment. These are clearer for us, and he is not to be followed as a critic of folklore. But the devils in character were his chief concern—and these abide. In the Wartburg he may have thrown an inkwell at the imagined devil; but shall we, then, forget that in the Wartburg he translated the New Testament, an epoch-making, language-creating service?

Ewald M. Plass observes, in his insightful *This Is Luther,* that it is unnecessary to determine the historicity of the inkwell-throwing incident, for it would have been highly characteristic of Luther, with his hell-defying courage, to have done so. Most certainly, the devil would not let a spiritual movement of such significance as the Reformation pass without the severest opposition.

The Wesleyan Revival

The activities of John Wesley and his companions in the eighteenth century had a profound and permanent effect upon the course of Christianity. In 1729, John, his brother Charles, and a few companions at Oxford University began a program of studies and devotions that earned for them the name "The Holy Club." The group emphasized Christian commitment, with special attention to Communion and spiritual development. By the late 1730s, Wesley had strongly committed himself to evangelism, made a tour to America, had a remarkable spiritual experience at a Moravian worship service in London, and launched a vigorous ministry of preaching and writing. The Methodist movement was underway.

For another half-century, Wesley and such colleagues as his brother Charles, George Whitefield, and William Grimshaw worked tirelessly, and saw much fruit of their labors. Wesley himself traveled some 250,000 miles in the British Isles, and preached between 40,000 and 50,000 sermons, often to crowds in the thousands. It has been said that the Wesleyan revival in England also preserved that country from civil war on the order of the French Revolution.

The revival did not go unnoticed, encountering the same opposition that other renewal movements had met. The satanic efforts were direct and physical for the most part, but there was also an upsurge of a bizarre strain of satanism. It was a cynical, parlor-type renunciation of Christian principles, which may simply have coincided with the Methodist revival. But it was, we can be sure, a satanic spirit in response to the moving of the Holy Spirit.

Among certain English aristocrats there arose a strange fascination with devil worship, human sacrifice, and the Black Mass—the inverting and profaning of the mass for evil purposes. In 1745, Sir Francis Dashwood and John Wilkes, cultured libertines, organized a "Hell Fire Club" in the old St.Mary's Abbey in Medmenham. The club, and others spawned by it, was devoted to sexual license and perversion, all in religious context, with obscene ceremonies, naked orgies, and devil worship. The members were all solemnly dedicated to Lucifer.

The blasphemous rakes usually secured virgins for their purposes, but girls from London brothels were also rented for their unspeakable orgies. The worship of Satan included the breaking of all of the Ten Commandments; taking the Sacrament from the naked bodies of women used as altars; and engaging in every conceivable form of perversion and debauchery.

The psychological toll was terrible. Some of the women went mad following the blasphemies; some of the men became old and impotent before they were thirty. The disgusting episode is but a historical curiosity today; but it shows to what extremes Satan will go in his convulsions against the Church of Jesus Christ.

The Present Circumstance

Having looked briefly at the Church's triumphs in the Apostolic, Reformation, and Wesleyan periods, we now come full circle to our own time again. Those are but three of many periods, incidentally, when Satan demonstrated his contempt for Christ and his opposition to His cause. In all periods, he has tried to scramble the process of divine worship. Now he is showing his hand again—more blatantly, perhaps, than in any but the Apostolic period. And it stands to reason that the greatest satanic opposition should be directed toward the beginning and closing periods of the Church. If that assumption is accurate, then religious confusion will increase in our time until the Lord shall return. Such is the repeated assertion of Scripture:

Now the Spirit speaketh expressly, that in the latter times some shall depart from the faith, giving heed to seducing spirits, and

doctrines of devils; Speaking lies in hypocrisy; having their conscience seared with a hot iron.

1 Timothy 4:1, 2

This know also, that in the last days perilous times shall come.

2 Timothy 3:1

But evil men and seducers shall wax worse and worse, deceiving,
and being deceived.

2 Timothy 3:13

Knowing this first, that there shall come in the *last days* scoffers,
walking after their own lusts.

2 Peter 3:3, emphasis added

How that they told you there should be mockers in the *last time,*
who should walk after their own ungodly lusts.

Jude 18, emphasis added

Not since the apostles ventured into an apostate, pagan,
occult world has there been a greater profusion of faiths bidding for the reverence of men. The devil has obviously re-
doubled his efforts in our time, with a full program of iniquity. We are told that he has a synagogue (Revelation 3:9),
with ministers, apostles, workers (2 Corinthians 11:13–15), a
doctrine (1 Timothy 4:1, 2), and a form of godliness (2 Timothy 3:5), and that he shall perform wonders and miracles
(Revelation 13:13, 14). The deceit embodied in these false-
hoods will become so rampant that the deceivers themselves
shall be deceived (2 Timothy 3:13), believing they have done
true service for Christ (Matthew 7:22, 23). The strategy behind this proliferation of false religion is two-fold: to win adherents to the false, and create doubt about the true.

The wonderful truth, however, is this: The same Scriptures that warn of Satan's tactics also reveal his ultimate failure. The Church that withstood all previous attacks will triumph, again, in this. Deceivers will be stopped in their
tracks (2 Timothy 3:9), and the Church will prevail against
all the powers of Satan.

13

More Than Conquerors

Paul had every reason to be dejected and bitter when he wrote his final letter to his young friend, Timothy. The aged apostle was in a Roman dungeon awaiting execution—not for any wrong he had done, but for preaching the Gospel of Christ. And yet, instead of showing defeat, his letter is upbeat in every way. The gloom of the Mamertine Prison, hard against the Roman Forum, did not penetrate the spirits of the dauntless Christian.

This is what he said: "For God hath not given us the spirit of fear; but of power, and of love, and of a sound mind" (2 Timothy 1:7).

Paul, who had suffered the worst of Satan's efforts against Christians, was fully aware of present and future dangers, but was nowise intimidated by them. He spoke of perilous times to come, reviewed the persecutions he had experienced, and directed his friend to the assurance of the holy Scriptures (2 Timothy 3:1–17). There is no provision for hangdog Christians anywhere in God's Word. We are expected to live positively and triumphantly, without intimidation by the devil.

As Jesus was victorious over all the power of evil, so His followers should be today. He has provided such grace for us that we can triumph over every device of evil—and more. We can by faith in Christ be more than just conquerors of sin—we can exercise mastery over the works of the devil. That is His unequivocal promise to us in Romans 8:35–39, where appears a catalog of about sixteen hostile powers that war against the spiritual life. These range from violence and martyrdom to the opposition of Satan through his angels, principalities, powers, things present, and things to come. The unmistakable, unchangeable assurance of God's Word, though, is that "in all these things we are more than conquerors through him that loved us" (Romans 8:37).

It is significant that we are *more than conquerors*. We not only gain victory over evil, but we live in mastery over it. We have not merely escaped the devil by the skin of our teeth—we are his superiors through Jesus Christ.

The Power of Hope

Looking further at Paul's predicament, we see a man who, facing almost certain death, possessed—and was possessed by—irrepressible hope. This, despite the fact that he foresaw the apostasy of the last days (2 Timothy 4:3, 4), and knew that an executioner's sword awaited him: "For I am now ready to be offered, and the time of my departure is at hand. I have fought a good fight, I have finished my course, I have kept the faith" (2 Timothy 4:6, 7).

Even the awareness of impending death could not daunt his hope; instead of fearing the sword, he anticipated a crown of righteousness. "Henceforth there is laid up for me a crown of righteousness, which the Lord, the righteous judge, shall give me at that day: and not to me only, but unto all them also that love his appearing" (2 Timothy 4:8).

Christ came to bring man hope, a gift Satan has never managed to give his followers (Ephesians 2:12; Hebrews 10:23). A Christian's hope is called "an anchor of the soul, both sure and stedfast" (Hebrews 6:19). Believers in Christ are saved by hope (Romans 8:24); they live by hope (1 Corinthians 13:13); and they are sustained by hope in suffering and death (1 Corinthians 15:19; 1 Thessalonians 4:13).

Hope is not the same as wishful thinking, though. It is a distinctly Christian attribute, a real and fortifying power in the Christian life. Before Christ, there was little hope in the world. Without Christ today, there is little hope in this life—and none for the life to come. In Dante's *Inferno,* these dreadful words appear over the portal of hell:

> Through me you pass into the city of woe:
> Through me you pass into eternal pain:
> Through me among the people lost for aye.
>
> Before me things create were none, save things
> Eternal, and eternal I endure.
> All hope abandon, ye who enter here.
>
> Dante
> *The Divine Comedy*

Hopelessness is the work of Satan, the curse of the wicked. It is not so with us who believe, for we have dwelling in us the living Christ, who is the hope of glory (Colossians 1:27).

Christ in You

Satan is no more a match for a child of God than he was for Jesus Christ. That is not a presumptuous statement, though it may seem so at first glance, but rather a reasonable statement of faith. The Christian is not alone, for he stands with Christ in spiritual warfare. We who are in Christ are never alone: Our lives are not centered in a philosophy, a doctrine, or a creed, but in the person, Jesus Christ. He is the center and circumference of the Christian life, which is not experienced by learning His teachings, but by receiving Him as Savior and serving Him as Lord.

Scripture repeatedly affirms that we are in Christ. In his excellent study of the Apostle Paul, *A Man in Christ,* James S. Stewart tabulates that the apostle spoke 164 times of being in Christ.

> I knew a man in Christ above fourteen years ago, (whether in the body, I cannot tell; or whether out of the body, I cannot tell: God knoweth;) such an one caught up to the third heaven.
>
> 2 Corinthians 12:2

I am crucified with Christ: nevertheless I live; yet not I, but Christ liveth in me: and the life which I now live in the flesh I live by the faith of the Son of God, who loved me, and gave himself for me.

Galatians 2:20

Therefore if any man *be* in Christ, he *is* a new creature: old things are passed away; behold, all things are become new.

2 Corinthians 5:17

Before leaving His disciples, Jesus made this promise to them, that they were in Him and He in them. "Abide in me and I in you. As the branch cannot bear fruit of itself, except it abide in the vine; no more can ye, except ye abide in me" (John 15:4). This assurance of togetherness with Christ was enough to sustain the apostles for as long as they lived. And the same promise, extended to us, is enough to sustain us. It speaks primarily of Christ as the source of a productive life, but it speaks equally of the security and assurance of His presence. Any experience of life, any harm or hurt that He would not allow for Himself He will not allow for us.

Security From the Devil

This section brings me back to one of the saddest fears among Christians today—that of being beset by demonic power. The fear often issues from the false premise that all sickness is caused by demonic presence, which leads to the tragic and totally false assumption that Satan has the power to possess whom he will. The fear also casts doubt, of course, on Christ's power to protect His own.

One of the most reassuring facts of the Christian life is that Jesus indwells His followers, and shares intimate communion with them (Revelation 3:20). The Lord will not share that communion with the devil, so it follows that no demon can invade any heart that belongs to Christ. Christians are "the temple of the living God; as God hath said, I will dwell in them, and walk in them; and I will be their

God, and they shall be my people" (2 Corinthians 6:16).

The imagery here is as beautiful as it is powerful. Christ is seen as a friend or guest indwelling those who accept Him, sharing the delights of life with them, enriching them with the manifold blessings of His presence. We read in the New Testament of the many homes He visited on earth, those of Mary, Martha and Lazarus, Simon the leper, and others— and in all of them He bestowed some largesse of His grace. He healed the sick, restored the dead to life, provided material needs, forgave sin, and—most important of all—shared the precious Word.

It follows that He also secures the home—or, in modern context, the heart—He indwells from all unwelcome or unholy intrusions. The presence of Jesus is the Christian's guarantee of security and blessedness.

One of the unequivocal statements of Scripture is this: "Ye are of God, little children, and have overcome them: because *greater is he that is in you, than he that is in the world*" (1 John 4:4, emphasis added). He that is in us is Jesus Christ, and he that is in the world is Satan. A similar, equally strong pronouncement was made by Christ to a group of Jews that questioned whether He was the Messiah. He said, "Ye believe not, because ye are not of my sheep," and he continued, with repetition and emphasis:

> My sheep hear my voice, and I know them, and they follow me: And I give unto them eternal life; and they shall never perish, neither shall any man pluck them out of my hand. My Father, which gave them me, is greater than all; and no man is able to pluck them out of my Father's hand. I and my Father are one.
>
> John 10:27–30

As Jesus defeated the devil in every personal encounter, so He defeats him now in the lives of Christian believers. He emphasized that "when a strong man armed keepeth his palace, his goods are in peace" (Luke 11:21). When He is in us, He keeps us secure from the abductions of Satan.

And that is true of both soul and body. The body of a Christian is a temple, not of Satan, but of the Holy Spirit (1 Corinthians 6:19, 20). This does not mean that Christians cannot be afflicted. Of course they can be, and they also die. What it does mean is that disease in a Christian is not demon-possession, but some physical disorder explainable in terms of the natural world.

Matthew 12:43–45 suggests, unfortunately, to some sincere Christians that Satan can repossess them even though they are servants of Christ. So, let us read the Scripture carefully:

When the unclean spirit is gone out of a man, he walketh through dry places, seeking rest, and findeth none. Then he saith, I will return into my house from whence I came out; and when he is come, he findeth it empty, swept, and garnished. Then goeth he, and taketh with himself seven other spirits more wicked than himself, and they enter in and dwell there: and the last state of that man is worse than the first. Even so shall it be also unto this wicked generation.

                                                        Matthew 12:43–45

This does not refer to a man who has given his life to Christ, but to one who evidently attempted, as the saying goes, to turn over a new leaf. The demon was not cast out by force, he *came out* voluntarily. He continued to speak of the man's heart as *my house,* however, and returned at will, because the heart was only *empty, swept, and garnished,* not occupied by Christ. Had Christ been in the man's heart, there is no way that the demon could have re-entered it—not even if he had brought a thousand fellow demons with him!

Paul, too, was bothered with a thorn in the flesh, apparently some physical disorder (probably an eye affliction), which he called a "messenger of Satan to buffet me" (2 Corinthians 12:7). He was buffeted, as a ship is buffeted by waves, but not possessed. In the same way, Jesus was crucified, even pierced, but by no means possessed. Those who belong to Christ can be claimed by no other.

The Sure Foundation

One of the unhappy predictions of Scripture concerns the apostasy and spiritual defection of the last days. Although defection existed in apostolic times (Acts 20:29, 30; 1 Timothy 5:15), it will be intensified as we near the end of the age. John called defection an anti-Christian spirit among men that were never really a part of the truth (1 John 2:18, 19).

The true Christian who sees these betrayals all around him is apt to fear that the foundations are eroding under him. That is only an illusion: Our foundation is steadfast and sure. Paul, writing to Timothy from prison, mentioned the apostasy of two men, Hymenaeus and Philetus, who erred concerning the truth: "Nevertheless," he encouraged his young friend, "the foundation of God standeth sure, having this seal, The Lord knoweth them that are his. And, Let every one that nameth the name of Christ depart from iniquity" (2 Timothy 2:19).

Not all who hear the Gospel will believe it, and not all who appear to believe will have a true, undergirding faith. Simon Magus was one such spurious believer. So were Hymenaeus and Philetus and Demas and the Nicolaitanes and the woman called Jezebel. But the unbelief of some does not "make the faith of God without effect. God forbid: yea, let God be true, but every man a liar . . ." (Romans 3:3, 4). God's Word to man is the believer's surest foundation. Those who keep it are secure from all workers of iniquity—those alive now and those yet to come.

Prove All Things

The position of believers will be secured by faith in Jesus Christ. There will be so many false Christs, and the Christian name will be used so falsely, that many will be confused. But there is one sure way to know the deceivers: They cannot live the life of Christ; they cannot truly show His spirit. It is indeed not by their claims, but by their fruits that we shall know them (Matthew 7:15–20).

Christian love "believeth all things" (1 Corinthians 13:7), but that is not the same as gullibility. We must believe what is in Scripture; we must believe the good in our brethren; but we must measure all things by the truth of Jesus Christ. "Prove all things; hold fast to that which is good" (1 Thessalonians 5:21). The Christian life must exist by the Word and by the Spirit of Christ, holding to the true and discarding the false.

Jesus in Revelation 2:2 commended the Ephesian Christians because they "tried them which say they are apostles, and are not, and . . . found them liars."

Paul warned the Galatians that there were some who "would pervert the gospel of Christ," and strongly admonished that if he, or even an angel, should "preach any other gospel unto you than that which we have preached unto you, let him be accursed" (Galatians 1:8). We should measure all dogma and every claim by the truth of God's Word.

John warned Christians not to believe every spirit, but to "try the spirits whether they are of God: because many false prophets are gone out into the world" (1 John 4:1).

Paul also directed the Corinthians to "Examine yourselves, whether ye be in the faith; prove your own selves . . ." (2 Corinthians 13:5). We who are called upon to prove all things should begin by examining our own faith, to determine whether it is truly in the person of Jesus Christ as revealed in Scripture. We must measure every doctrine and belief by the evidence of Scripture.

Contend for the Faith

The short Epistle of Jude takes a careful view of the last-days apostasy, with the encouragement of Christians its principal purpose. In this brief message of warning and edification, which is as cogent as it is concise, Jude exhorted the body of believers to "earnestly *contend for the faith* . . . once de-livered unto the saints" (verse 3, emphasis added). The word *contend* is a verb of strength, signifying the utmost effort of the will, an exertion of muscle and nerve to resist all challenges. It suggests determination to hold a position under attack by an adversary—and if we must contend for the faith of Christ, it is because that faith is under attack by adverse in-fluences.

In his powerful tract, Jude enumerates seven destructive forces that are arrayed against the Christian faith of love and purity. He warns against the murmuring spirit of Israel, who complained when God did not perform according to their ideas; the rebellion of fallen angels, who were more loyal to Lucifer than to God; the perversions of Sodom, where human nature was changed from something beautiful into something sordid; the despisers of authority, who recognize no restraints or regulations in life; the self-will of Cain, who wanted to substitute his form of worship for God's; the greed of Balaam, who used his gifts to make personal gain; and the usurpation of Core (Korah), who defied the leadership of God's servant, Moses.

In every one of these enemies of the faith we see the hand of Satan, who uses the devices of complaining and rebellion against God, carnal perversion, spiritual perversity, self-will, material greed, and usurpation of authority to gain his ob-jectives.

Jude also counsels on how to preserve the true faith in the midst of such treacherous forces. He states that we must build ourselves up in the most holy faith, upon the Lord Jesus Christ and His eternal Word (Jude 20). The founda-tion of Christ will stand forever, so that those who build upon Him need have no fear of falling.

We are exhorted to pray in the Holy Ghost, keep ourselves in the love of God, and look for the mercy of our Lord Jesus Christ, which will preserve us unto eternal life. The faith of Jesus Christ is our foundation, and our bulwark against all

the attacks of Satan. It is final truth, which admits no addition or subtraction, by which we are kept for Jesus Christ.

Resist the Devil

A man in Christ is more than a match for the powers of
evil. He can overcome; he can live triumphantly. The devil is
limited in his powers, although he tries to appear more powerful than he is. We must not be intimidated by his threats,
but recall the words of James: "Submit yourselves therefore
to God. *Resist the devil, and he will flee from you*" (James 4:7,
emphasis added). Be aware, however, that our successful resistance of the devil hinges on our submission to God.

Satan is similar to the puff adder I once encountered in a
field near my boyhood home. Startled by my approach, the
snake puffed itself into a fearsome shape, and made sinuous,
threatening motions. His bluff worked on me. I recall now
with chagrin how I ran from it as rapidly as my childish legs
would take me, abandoning the field to it. I need not have: If
I had challenged the adder's right to my father's field, it
would have been it that would have fled, for the snake was
no match for me.

I have always remembered that. No Christian should ever
desert his Father's field because of fear of Satan. If we resist
him in the power of Christ, it is he who will do the fleeing.

We can learn two important lessons when we consider
Satan's power with that of the Holy Spirit. First, *there are defi-
nite limits on Satan's influence* upon Christian believers. Having
done all he can, he still falls far short of real harm to the
cause of Christ. He must then resort to bluff and threat of
menace, like the adder in my father's field.

Second, we see God's people triumph over all evil circumstances. We are more than victors in battle, more than conquerors in conflict; we reign through Christ over all circumstances of life. Even suffering for His name magnifies our

witness, and drives us closer to His side. Where Christians have taken their stand without fear or apology, there the devil has mocked them, ridiculed them, has even flung his darts at them. But he has never conquered them.

And he never will.

PART IV
The Triumph of God

14

Triumph in Christ

Despite the growing spiritual tension of our time; despite the storm of apostasy and increase of demonic activity, Christians can take heart in the fact that Satan is a conquered foe. In a cosmic sense, he is already defeated and has no chance of reversing our victory. This does not mean, however, that he has admitted defeat, or that he will slacken his efforts to wrest victory from approaching doom. Indeed, he will intensify his efforts to unprecedented proportions as his days grow shorter, and his final, desperate drive for victory will make the last days extremely dangerous for mankind. And, although the cosmic issue has already been determined, multitudes of individuals will be deceived and destroyed before the literal demise of Satan is accomplished.

Certain Victory

There are evidences that Satan knows that his is a lost cause but—hoping for reprieve—will pour more and more evil and deception into our generation. Christians need not be dismayed or bewildered by the turmoil to come, for we have advance knowledge of what will happen. God, by revelation of His Word, has shown believers what evil will occur and exactly what the results will be. Consequently, he expects us to be enlightened and unafraid, not in the dark and filled with dread. So, keep courage as the distress increases, and know that one thing is certain: God and His righteous cause shall triumph. *The devil cannot win.*

In the beginning, the devil set out to take the place of God, a mad scheme he has never abandoned. Insane as that ambition may seem today, we must remember that he has followed it doggedly through the ages, and he will follow it to the end. We must also remember that modern satanists, witches, false prophets, and workers of iniquity would prefer Satan to God as the supreme being in the universe. This evil company, along with the host of demons that have followed Satan from the beginning, make for a considerable body of supporters. And as this following grows larger and more militant, the peril will increase.

That Satan foresees his eventual defeat is suggested in such words as "he knoweth that he hath but a short time" (Revelation 12:12). This awareness will not diminish Satan's wrath, however, but will rather increase it. He sees the heavy odds against him, and is all the more desperate and dogged because of it. He knows the doom that awaits him if he fails, and this spurs him to maddening intensity.

Perhaps I can illustrate the situation. A skilled chess player can usually tell long before the competition ends whether he will lose the match. He knows when he has made a critical error, unrecognized by casual observers, that will tip the odds away from him. Barring some major error by his opponent that could give reprieve, the challenger knows he can only lose in the end. His cleverest moves may delay defeat, but nothing can prevent it. He doesn't stop, however, but all the more grimly takes what men he can from his victorious opponent, hoping against hope to pull victory from defeat.

I don't mean to compare the serious, devilish intent of Satan with a chess game; certainly, the analogy is imperfect. So let me mention a brutal, deadly, much more appropriate circumstance of desperation.

Long before the Allied armies invaded the German Fatherland in World War II, Hitler and his military leaders knew that their campaign was a lost cause. A few of the wisest generals realized the Nazis had lost the war even before the Allied invasion of Normandy on D-Day. But the dull awareness of eventual defeat did not end the Nazi madness. Indeed, some of the greatest havoc and destruction came *after* the end was in sight. The Wehrmacht fought fiercely, hoping by daring, desperate assaults, and military cunning to snatch victory from the jaws of defeat. Consequently, thousands of persons, military and civilian, were senselessly killed long after the outcome was a foregone conclusion.

It will be the same in God's conflict with Satan. To believers, there is no question about the outcome; but Satan will do much damage among those who do not have the security of Christ or the knowledge of His Word.

Christ's Victory

It was Christ who gained the victory over the devil, and all previous and subsequent victories by God's people were premised upon His triumph. We read of Old Testament patriarchs and prophets who won stunning victories over the devil's finest representatives. Probably the best known of these were Moses and Elijah—at least, their exploits were certainly the most graphic and dramatic.

Moses was challenged by the sorcery of Jannes and Jambres, court sorcerers to the Pharaoh, who imitated the Hebrew deliverer's spiritual power. The challenge resulted in one of the most remarkable spiritual victories in Hebrew history (Exodus 7:10–12; 2 Timothy 3:8), leading, ultimately, to the deliverance of Israel from slavery in Egypt. Possibly even more dramatic was Elijah's victory over the pagan abominations of Baal (1 Kings 18:25–40): The holy prophet's courage and faith, which resulted in the annihilation of 850 pagan prophets, touched a rare peak of Jewish spirituality.

Although the triumphs of Moses and Elijah occurred long before Christ lived, they were actually pre-Christian demonstrations of Christ's power over Satan. Both men appeared in

vision at the Transfiguration of Christ, in homage to Him
and deference to His divinity (Matthew 17:2, 3). Of Moses, it
is specifically stated that his victorious life was predicated
upon the person of Christ—even though Moses lived two
thousand years before Christ:

> By faith Moses, when he was come to years, refused to be called
> the son of Pharaoh's daughter; Choosing rather to suffer affliction
> with the people of God, than to enjoy the pleasures of sin for a sea-
> son; Esteeming the reproach *of Christ* greater riches than the trea-
> sures in Egypt. . . .
>
> Hebrews 11:24–26, emphasis added

Jesus was born into a world dominated by Satan, the civilized as well as the barbarian lands (2 Corinthians 4:4; 1
John 5:19 Revised Standard Version); despite their cultural
advancement, the Greeks, Romans, and peoples of other advanced nations lived in spiritual alienation from God. Christ
came to lead men back to the Father by destroying the
devil's work (1 John 3:8), and providing a basis for human
victory over evil (John 16:33; 17:14–16). His advent on
earth, at the peak of Satan's influence and at the nadir of
human experience, was the pivotal point of human history.
The devil fought Him all the way, in every way, for—if he
were to succeed in his mad ambition—Satan knew he must
by all means overcome Christ. He therefore tried to kill Him
as an infant (Matthew 2:16), and again at the outset of His
ministry (Luke 4:28, 29); tempted Him to profane His ministry (Luke 4:1–13); tried to preempt and corrupt His accla-
mation as the Son of God (Mark 1:24, 25, 34; 3:11, 12); and
finally had Him ignominiously betrayed, deserted, denied,
and killed (Luke 22:3, 31; Mark 14:50, 70; Mark 15:25–37).

For a short time, it seemed that the devil had succeeded.
But not so, for Jesus rose from death in final triumph. It is
difficult for the mortal mind to grasp the magnitude of
Christ's Resurrection from death, which forever sealed the
doom of Satan. From the time Jesus came out of the tomb,

He was no longer within reach of Satan: The triumph of God was perfected in all points. The devil lost all hope of success when he found that even death could not prevail against the power of God (Colossians 2:14, 15).

His hatred of and determination against Christ turned the devil into the instrument of his own defeat. For instance, the blood of Christ became the means of man's redemption (Ephesians 1:7). The devil added pain to Christ by having Him scourged, only to see those stripes become the source of human healing (1 Peter 2:24). He sought to compound the humiliation of crucifixion by flanking Christ with two thieves, only to lose one of them to Christ (Luke 23:43). The Crucifixion of Christ was Satan's biggest blunder; the Resurrection, his greatest defeat. Christ submitted to the ignominious treatment willingly, so that through death He might destroy him that had the power of death—that is, the devil (Hebrews 2:14).

Because Christ triumphed over death, which is the masterwork of Satan, the tempter's greatest power has been eliminated. Until Christ rose from death, the great pessimism of all men centered on death or the fear of death: The literature of ancient man reflects a pervading fatalism, with the grave viewed as the dead end of human experience. When Christ emerged from the tomb, He wrested forever from Satan his ultimate device of fear: Thereafter, followers of Christ would know that even the fact of death is not defeat. Death is not the cessation of life, but merely a change from one sphere of existence to another.

He that believeth on the Son hath everlasting life. . . .

John 3:36

He that heareth my word, and believeth on him that sent me, hath everlasting life. . . .

John 5:24

Verily, verily, I say unto you, He that believeth on me hath everlasting life.

John 6:47

I am the resurrection, and the life: he that believeth in me, though he were dead, yet shall he live.

John 11:25

God hath given to us eternal life, and this life is in his Son. He that hath the Son hath life; and he that hath not the Son of God hath not life.

1 John 5:11, 12

Individual Triumph

In Christ's death, believers have victory over sin; in His Resurrection, they have victory over death. With Satan's power thus broken, believers can enjoy victory, through Christ's undisputed dominion over sin and death (Romans 6:5–13). It is important, however, that Christians always remember they are dependent upon Christ in all things, as did Paul: "I can do all things through Christ which strengtheneth me" (Philippians 4:13).

By the power of Christ we can triumph over anything the devil can bring against us. We are not promised immunity from pain or death, but freedom from the dominion of Satan, security from his power over men, and assurance of life eternal. As Paul wrote, "It is a faithful saying: For if we be dead with him, we shall also live with him: If we suffer, we shall also reign with him: if we deny him, he also will deny us" (2 Timothy 2:11, 12).

It is inappropriate, then, for Christians to lead hangdog, browbeaten, downtrodden lives. That kind of fatalistic behavior is appropriate to the vanquished, the losers—but we who are in Christ are as certain of triumph as is Christ whom we serve. In time to come, believers in Him shall reign with Him over Satan and all his works (Revelation 5:10).

But that is moving ahead of the sequence of Scripture. First, there will be a time of trouble and tribulation, culminating in the demise of Satan.

15

The Demise of Satan

Among his illustrations for Dante's *Inferno*, Gustave Doré, the gifted French artist of the past century, included an unforgettable drawing of Lucifer in the caverns of hell. It struck me forcibly as a child. It still does. The brooding form of the devil is seen dimly through the infernal gloom: scowling, malevolent, inscrutably evil and cunning, the remorseless lord of the underworld. Framed in a curtain of jagged stalactites and massive boulders, among which lie the tortured inmates of his hell, the monstrous, bat-winged father of evil sits glowering in the sullen blackness.

But no representation of Satan, impressive and terrible as it may be, can adequately portray the concentrated evil of the fallen angel, once perfect in wisdom and beauty—though Doré came as close as anyone I know of. Human skill can no more sketch the evil visage of Satan than human genius can comprehend his evil character. His scheme of dominion has brought us down to these days of peril and distress. He will be in hell one day, as we are assured by the holy Scriptures, but he is loose and on a rampage in this present time.

The Latter Days

The days immediately ahead will reveal to the world much more of Satan's infinite capacity for evil. But they will even more clearly reveal the triumphant power of God. There will exist simultaneously a steadfast faith in some and spiritual apostasy in others, a situation frequently foretold in the Scriptures. Peter, on the Day of Pentecost, spoke of a *last days* outpouring of the Spirit (Acts 2:17); Paul, on the other hand, wrote of a *latter times* departure from the faith (1 Timothy 4:1, 2). It has been the contemporary spiritual outpouring that has induced the counteracting surge of iniquity; now it has become necessary for the Holy Spirit to restrain the works of Satan. For only the power of the Spirit can check the power of evil in the last days.

Except for the presence of the Holy Spirit in God's people, the world would soon be overrun with Charles Mansons, Idi Amins, Jim Joneses, "Children of God," Father Divines, Hitlers, Stalins, and worse. Much worse. Yes, worse men than these shall soon arise, as part of an attempted takeover by the anti-Christ influences. Iniquity and spiritual deception will become so unrestrained that even the staunchest Christians will be in danger of confusion. "There shall be false teachers among you, who privily shall bring in damnable heresies, even denying the Lord that bought them, and bring upon themselves swift destruction. And many shall follow their pernicious ways . . ." (2 Peter 2:1, 2).

When the chaos comes, we should not be overcome, for it will tell Christians that Satan is in his final spasm of fury: His demise is near. As Peter said, those who trust in Christ have no need to fear, for "The Lord knoweth how to deliver the godly out of temptations . . ." (2 Peter 2:9). Jude, regarding the same period of apostasy, added, "Now unto him that is able to keep you from falling, and to present you faultless before the presence of his glory with exceeding joy" (Jude 24).

To that assurance, Christians say, "Amen." Amen, both now and forever. The assurance of watchcare does not, however, extend to those who reject Christ, of whom it is said, "Evil men and seducers shall wax worse and worse, deceiving, and being deceived" (2 Timothy 3:13).

The Great Tribulation

Wickedness in the last days will progress into disorder of every sort—moral, spiritual, political, material, economic—

so that no one alive will be able to fully escape its effects. This time of worldwide distress is known in prophetic language as the Great Tribulation: "For then shall be great tribulation, such as was not since the beginning of the world to this time, no, nor ever shall be" (Matthew 24:21).

The time shall be one of such peril, such misery, such depression, that, immediately prior to it, Christ will gather His followers from the earth to Himself in the air. This great miracle of redemption and deliverance is known by believers as the Rapture—the spiriting away of those who are Christ's. Although the word *rapture* is not used in Scripture, its reality is spoken of frequently:

> Because thou hast kept the word of my patience, I also will keep thee from the hour of temptation, which shall come upon all the world, to try them that dwell upon the earth.
>
> Revelation 3:10

> For the Lord himself shall descend from heaven with a shout, with the voice of the archangel, and with the trump of God: and the dead in Christ shall rise first: Then we which are alive and remain shall be caught up together with them in the clouds, to meet the Lord in the air: and so shall we ever be with the Lord.
>
> 1 Thessalonians 4:16, 17

With Christians removed from the scene, the work of iniquity will be fully revealed upon the earth (2 Thessalonians 2:7). At first there will be false peace and prosperity, which will serve only to disguise the true condition of the world, and lull those who missed the Rapture into a deceptive sense of well-being. Then the evil will break forth. With the restraining power of the Holy Spirit no longer a hindrance to the powers of evil, disorder and desolation will run riot throughout the world. There will be political anarchy, accompanied by economic recession deepening to depression and finally to panic. And most of the terrors of this dreadful period, unprecedented and indescribable, will relate to Satan's being cast upon the earth during the Tribulation:

And the great dragon was cast out, that old serpent, called the Devil, and Satan, which deceiveth the whole world: he was cast out into the earth, and his angels were cast out with him. . . . Therefore rejoice, ye heavens, and ye that dwell in them. Woe to the inhabiters of the earth and of the sea! for the devil is come down unto you, having great wrath, because he knoweth that he hath but a short time.

Revelation 12:9, 12

The prince of the power of the air, furious in the knowledge that his demise has already begun, will unleash the full measure of his wrath upon the world. His fury will be especially directed toward the Jews, whom he has long hated, and toward those who turned to Christ during the Tribulation (Revelation 12:13–17). In a paroxysm of rage, still hoping somehow to avoid the waiting pit, Satan will be all the more vicious and destructive.

The Antichrist

During this miserable, chaotic period, the devil will carry his scheme of usurpation to its horrendous end. Two men— one political, the other religious—will embody the spirit, nature, and power of Satan. The ultimate iniquity will come when a world leader emerges with political skills that gain the admiration of the world. Where there is threat of war, he will show the way to peace; where there is financial panic, he will show the way to prosperity; where there are shortages of food and provisions, he will show the way to plenty (Daniel 8:23–25; Revelation 13:1–7). He will become a world dictator, with all nations subject to him and his policies.

The Bible speaks of that man as the beast. We know him as the Antichrist.

Through Satan's power, the Antichrist will perform great wonders and miracles (Revelation 13:3, 4), with the result that both Satan and Antichrist will be worshipped by the world. Only those who know the way of Christ and turn to

Him at that late hour will refuse to engage in such worship. The beast, following the pattern of his god, Satan, will exalt himself above all that is called God, or that is worshipped; that is, he will proclaim himself to be God. As a result of his power, his signs, lying wonders, and counterfeit righteousness, men will believe his lies unto their own damnation (2 Thessalonians 2:4–12).

The second beast, called the False Prophet—the third member of the unholy trinity—will serve the purposes of Satan and the Antichrist. This religious leader will compel men, upon threat of death, to worship the beast (Revelation 13:15). It is significant that Lucifer's aspirations in the earliest ages will still prevail at the end of his deceitful career. Still imitating God all the way, he will head this trinity of iniquity, and will perform miracles; restore life to the Antichrist after he has received a deadly wound; make an image live; and generally pretend to the world that he is God.

Lucifer, the creature who wanted to be God, will thus pursue his rebellious scheme to its calamitous end.

Satan Bound

The Tribulation period, according to computations in Daniel 9, will last for seven years. Seven years are but a short period in the long and sinister history of Satan, but for those who live in them, they will seem an eternity.

At the end of the seven years, Christ and His raptured saints will return to the earth to set up a thousand-year kingdom of righteousness, known in prophetic study as the Millennium (Revelation 19:11–16). This is that Second Coming of Christ spoken of in Scripture as a time of retribution and judgment upon the ungodly (Matthew 24:29–31; Luke 21:25–27; 2 Thessalonians 1:7–10; 2:1–3, 8; Jude 14, 15).

The Antichrist and False Prophet shall at that time be cast alive into a lake of fire burning with brimstone. The evil of these men shall be so great that they will go straight into hell, without the intermediate stage of death (Revelation 19:20). While the Antichrist and False Prophet, political and religious partners of Satan, receive immediate judgment and eternal damnation, Satan shall, for reasons we shall learn, be bound in chains and consigned to the bottomless pit for a thousand years. An angel of the Lord will lay "hold on the dragon, that old serpent, which is the Devil, and Satan, and [will bind] him a thousand years, And cast him into the bottomless pit, and shut him up, and set a seal upon him, that he should deceive the nations no more, till the thousand years should be fulfilled: and after that he must be loosed a little season" (Revelation 20:2, 3). The bottomless pit is an intermediate stage of hell, reached prior to the lake of eternal fire. Notice that it is an angel that binds the devil and casts him into the bottomless pit, demonstrating that even angels are more powerful than Satan. He who undertook to replace God will find himself inferior to God's angelic creation. During the Millennium, with Satan bound and his agents annihilated, the earth will know a peace and tranquillity it has not known since Satan beguiled Adam and Eve in the Garden of Eden.

Satan's End

When the Lord returns to earth to take vengeance upon His adversaries and establish the millennial kingdom, most of the people on earth will be in league with Satan. These shall be ruled "with a rod of iron" during the thousand years, with no occasion to exercise their allegiance to Satan. Subdued but not changed in heart, those evil-hearted persons shall live like fifth columnists among the saints of God.

The self-styled beast, Allister Crowley, whose evil is mentioned in an earlier chapter, anticipated Satan's overthrow of God in the final conflict and pledged his assistance to that end. He expressed belief that the devil would be victorious, and declared his preference of him to Jesus Christ. There will be many other evil persons of similar mind.

At the end of his thousand years' imprisonment in the bottomless pit, Satan will again be released. Evil as ever, he will immediately resume his activities against the people of God (Revelation 20:7-9). And at that time, all the devil's fifth columnists will rally to his side in fatal allegiance. It seems strange to us, almost unbelievable, that anyone could possibly maintain such resistance to God and truth. But that, after all, is the example of the Evil One. If a thousand years in the bottomless pit will not change Satan, certainly a thousand years in enforced peace will not change his followers. The reason is "because they received not the love of the truth, that they might be saved. And for this cause God shall send them strong delusion, that they should believe a lie" (2 Thessalonians 2:10, 11).

The release of Satan from the bottomless pit will serve to gather in one place all remaining enemies of God and righteousness. Lucifer and his fallen angels and earthly minions will come together for a final, suicidal battle with God's people (Jude 6; Revelation 20:7, 8).

Early in Christian history, Augustine wrote in *The City of God:*

This, then, is his purpose in seducing them, to draw them to this battle. For even before this he was wont to use as many and various seductions as he could contrive. And the words, "he shall go out" mean, he shall burst forth from lurking hatred into open persecution. For this persecution, occurring while the final judgment is imminent, shall be the last which shall be endured by the holy Church throughout the world, the whole city of Christ being assailed by the whole city of the devil, as each exists on earth.

When this final separation of the tares from the wheat is made, fire will come down from God out of heaven and devour the workers of iniquity (Revelation 20:9). Then Satan—alone, unloved, unlamented, twisted with hate, rebellious to the end—will be cast into the everlasting fire prepared for him and his angels (Matthew 25:41).

Victory Forever

The spiritual victory introduced by the demise of Satan will be an eternal triumph of righteousness. So let us note with confidence and assurance the words that tell of proud Lucifer's end: "And the devil that deceived them was cast into the lake of fire and brimstone, where the beast and the false prophet are, and shall be tormented day and night for ever and ever" (Revelation 20:10). The lake of fire is not the kingdom of Satan, therefore, as human satirists would have it, but his eternal prison, his place of banishment in tortured and final defeat. Once cast into the lake of fire, the demise of Satan will be complete. Iniquity, rebellion, hate, and all evil will die with him.

In *Paradise Lost,* John Milton—with a seer's perception and a poet's license—expressed theological truth with poetic imagery:

> Hell at last
> Yawning received them whole, and on them closed
> Hell, their fit habitation, fraught with fire
> Unquenchable, the house of woe and pain.
> Disburdened Heaven rejoiced, and soon repaired
> Her mural breach, returning whence it rolled.
> Sole victor, from the expulsion of his foes,
> Messiah his triumphal chariot turned:
> To meet him all his saints, who silent stood
> Eye-witnesses of his almighty acts,
> With jubilee advanced.

> John Milton
> *Paradise Lost*

All influences that came into the world with Satan will leave the world with him: Sin, sorrow, sickness, and death will have no place in eternity. Paul, in his great rhapsody on eternal life, rejoiced that Christ "must reign, till he hath put all enemies under his feet. The last enemy that shall be destroyed is death" (1 Corinthians 15:25, 26). Every evil influence will pass into oblivion with Satan, so that God and man shall live forever in the fellowship He intended (Revelation 21:3).

As it was said in heaven when Satan was cast out, so let it be said on earth: Now is come salvation, and strength, and the kingdom of our God, and the power of His Christ: for the accuser of our brethren is cast down.

Therefore rejoice, O Earth; and all that dwell therein, rejoice.

Bibliography

Atkins, Susan, and Bob Slosser. *Child of Satan, Child of God.* Plainfield, New Jersey: Logos International, 1977.

Belford, Lee A. "Sun Myung Moon and the Unification Church," *Intellect,* 105 (April, 1977), 336.

Booth, Edwin P. *Martin Luther: Oak of Saxony.* New York: Round Table Press, 1933.

Bugliosi, Vincent, with Curt Gentry. *Helter Skelter.* New York: W. W. Norton, 1974.

Cary, Henry F. (trans.). *Dante Alighieri: The Divine Comedy.* New York: Crown Publishers, n.d.

Chafer, Lewis Sperry. *Satan.* Chicago: The Moody Press, 1919.

Cripps, Edward J. "Listening to Those Who Search," *America,* 135 (September 18, 1976), 147.

Crittenden, Ann. "The Incredible Story of Ann Gordon and Reverend Sun Myung Moon," *Good Housekeeping,* 183 (October, 1976), 86–100.

Dods, Marcus (trans.). *Augustine: The City of God.* New York: The Modern Library, Random House, 1950.

Donohoe, Tony. "A Weekend with the Moonies," *Intellect,* 105 (April, 1977), 338.

Durant, Will. "Our Oriental Heritage." Vol. I of *The Story of Civilization.* New York: Simon and Schuster, 1935.

————. "Caesar and Christ." Vol. III of *The Story of Civilization.* New York: Simon and Schuster, 1944.

Edersheim, Alfred. *The Life and Times of Jesus the Messiah.* 2 vols. Grand Rapids: Wm. Eerdmans, 1883.

Fuller, Christopher. "Cults on Campus," *Ladies' Home Journal* (May, 1979), 40.

Gaebelein, A. C. *Gabriel and Michael the Archangel.* Wheaton, Illinois: Van Kampen, 1945.

Harris, Sara. *Father Divine.* New York: Collier Books, 1953.

Hastings, James (ed.). *A Dictionary of the Apostolic Church.* 2 vols. New York: Scribner's, 1916.

Hopkins, Joseph M. "The Children of God: Disciples of Deception," *Christianity Today,* 21 (February 18, 1977), 18–23.

Hultquist, Lee. *They Followed the Piper.* Plainfield, New Jersey: Logos International, 1977.

"Hurry, My Children, Hurry," *Time,* 113 (March 26, 1979), 27–28.

Jennings, F. C. *Satan: His Person, Work, Place and Destiny.* Neptune, New Jersey: Loiseaux Brothers, 1975.

Kerns, Phil, with Doug Wead. *People's Temple—People's Tomb.* Plainfield, New Jersey: Logos International, 1979.

Kilduff, Marshall and Ron Javers. *The Suicide Cult.* New York: Bantam Books, 1978.

Krause, Charles A. *Guyana Massacre.* New York: Berkley Publishing Corporation, 1978.

Kyemba, Henry. *A State of Blood.* New York: Paddington Press, 1977.

Levitt, Zola. *The Spirit of the Sun Myung Moon.* Irvine, California: Harvest House Publishers, 1976.

Lochner, Louis P. (ed.) *The Goebbels Diaries.* New York: Doubleday, 1948.

Mannix, Daniel Pratt. *The Hell Fire Club.* New York: Ballantine Books, 1959.

Maple, Eric. *Witchcraft.* Hong Kong: Mandarin Publishers Limited, 1973.

Milton, John. *The Complete Poems of John Milton.* New York: Crown Publishers, 1936.

"Nightmare in Jonestown," *Time,* 112 (December 4, 1978), 16–27.

Outler, Albert C. (trans.). *Augustine: Confessions.* Philadelphia: Westminster Press, 1955.

Parker, Robert Allerton. *The Incredible Messiah, the Deification of Father Divine.* Boston: Little, Brown and Company, 1937.

Parkes, Henry Bamford. *A History of Mexico.* Boston: Houghton-Mifflin Company, 1950.

Pentecost, J. Dwight. *Your Adversary the Devil.* Grand Rapids: Zondervan Publishing House, 1969.

Plass, Ewald M. *This Is Luther.* St. Louis, Missouri: Concordia Publishing House, 1948.

Prescott, William H. *History of the Conquest of Mexico.* New York: The Modern Library, n.d.

Rubin, Arnold P. *Hitler and the Nazis—The Evil That Men Do.* New York: Bantam Books, 1977.

Schaff, Philip. *History of the Christian Church,* Vol. I. Grand Rapids: Eerdmans, 1910.

Shirer, William L. *The Rise and Fall of the Third Reich.* New York: Simon and Schuster, 1960.

Sontag, Frederick. *Sun Myung Moon and the Unification Church.* Nashville: Abingdon, 1977.

Sparks, Jack. *The Mind Benders.* Nashville: Thomas Nelson, 1977.

Stewart, James S. *A Man in Christ.* New York: Harper and Brothers, n.d.

"The Occult: A Substitute Faith," *Time,* 99 (June 19, 1972), 62–68.

Thiel, Rudolf. *Luther.* Philadelphia: Muhlenberg Press, 1955.

Tompkins, Peter. *Mysteries of the Mexican Pyramids.* New York: Harper and Row, 1976.

Unger, Merrill F. *Biblical Demonology.* Wheaton, Illinois: Van Kampen Press, 1952.

——————. *Demons in the World Today.* Wheaton, Illinois: Tyndale House Publishers, 1971.

Wallis, Wilson D. *Messiahs, Their Role in Civilization.* Washington: American Council on Public Affairs, 1943.

Westermarck, Edward. *The Origin and Development of the Moral Ideas.* Vol. I. London: Macmillan and Company, 1906.

White, John Wesley. *The Devil.* Wheaton, Illinois: Tyndale House Publishers, 1977.

Williams, Charles. *Witchcraft.* New York: Meridian Books, 1959.

Worsley, F. W. "Idolatry," James Hastings (ed.) *Dictionary of the Apostolic Church,* Vol. I. New York: Scribner's, 1916.